The Possibilities of Organization

by Barry Oshry

ISBN 0-910411-10-7

Table of Contents

INTRODUCTION

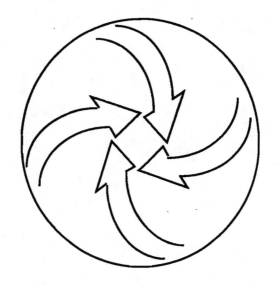

It is possible that I have observed more organizations in action, and have spoken with more people in organizations, than has any other human being.

Some of these organizations are like the ones you work in or are involved with: hospitals, universities, manufacturing plants, service organizations, religious institutions, high technology firms, schools, the military, government agencies, and so forth. Others are organizations I have created for a few hours, or a day, or for several days for the purpose of examining organizational processes more closely and deepening my and other's understanding of life in organizations.

This book is about ORGANIZATION as I have seen it and as it has been described to me. It is about ORGANIZATION: what it is and what its possibilities are. It is about ORGANIZATION as it is experienced in the 100 best-run companies and in large universities and in parish churches and in family-owned department stores.

It is about ORGANIZATION as it is experienced by ALL the players -- by people at the TOP, on the BOTTOM, and in the MIDDLE of organizations.

And it is about ORGANIZATION as it is experienced by people who are the CUSTOMERS of organizations.

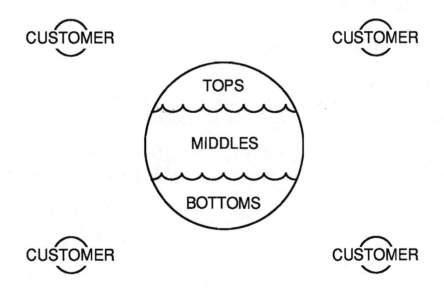

This book is about THEM: *those* TOPS, *those* BOTTOMS, *those* MIDDLES, and *those* CUSTOMERS *you* have to deal with.

And it is about YOU: *you* as a TOP, *you* as a BOTTOM, *you* as a MIDDLE, and *you* as a CUSTOMER, and the part you play in ORGANIZATION.

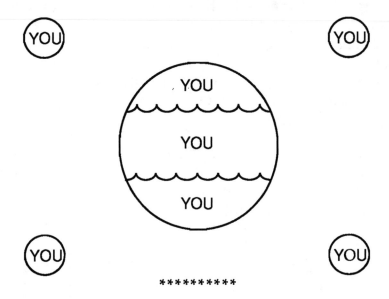

****

This book is not about competing in the marketplace, yet it opens up possibilities for competing more vigorously.

This book is not about manufacturing, yet it opens up possibilities for getting more and better products out the door.

This book is not about the bottom line, yet it opens up possibilities for greater profitability.

This book is not about turnover, absenteeism, and grievances, yet it opens up possibilities for greatly improved labor-management relationships.

This book is about the possibilities of ORGANIZATION -- about how it is and how it can be. And fundamentally, it is about what it takes to get from one to the other.

****

This book reads easily -- perhaps too easily. I suggest that you take your time with it, that you work with it, that you read it several times, that you discuss it with friends, with co-workers, that you use it to look deeply into your own experiences in ORGANIZATION.

My intention in this book is that *you will see ORGANIZATION more clearly than ever before*: what has made no sense to you will now make sense; mysteries will clear up; other people in the organization will appear in a new light.

And I have a still deeper purpose here: that, out of this clarity, new possibilities will open up for you, new ways for you to be in the organization, powerful ways, ways that will produce greater results for the organization and deeper satisfaction for you.

I am about to tell you the story of ORGANIZATION. The cat will soon be out of the bag. Once you understand this story, life in the organization can never be the same for you. You will see the story develop in your organization; you will understand *how* it goes the way it goes; you will see your part in the story; and you will see *choice*: to play out the familiar scenario or to create some other scenario, one that is more productive for you, more satisfying... and more challenging.

There is still time to put this book down. Once read, it is the end of organizational innocence.

Barry Oshry
Boston, Mass.

POSSIBILITY I:

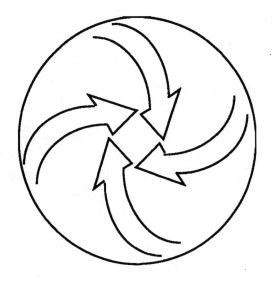

INTERNAL WARFARE

There is a story that happens with great

regularity in organizational life. It is a

story in which the organization goes to

war...with itself.

There is a story that develops with great regularity.

It is the story of an organization in its environment.

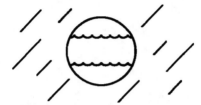

It is the story of an organization struggling to survive in a complex and changing world.

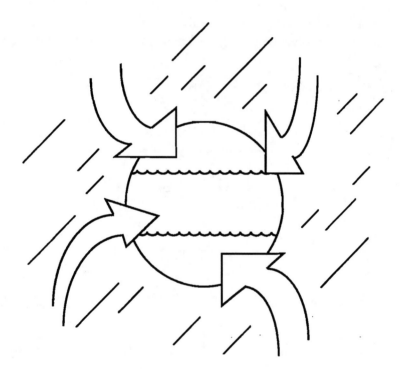

In the organization,

there are the Tops, who have overall responsibility for the organization;

there are the Bottoms, who do the work of the organization, producing its products or rendering its services;

and there are the Middles, who administer, manage, or supervise the work of others.

And in the environment, there are the Customers who look to the organization to provide them with products and services when they want them, to the quality they want them, and at a price they are willing to pay.

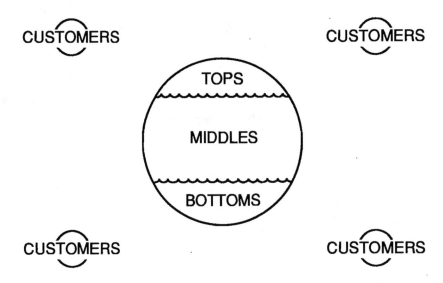

The organization is struggling to survive in a complex and changing world;

yet, in the midst of that struggle, the organization is at war with itself.

Tops are isolated and out of touch with much of the organization.

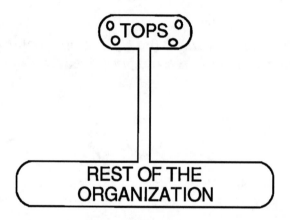

Bottoms are drawn together, feeling close to one another, and separate from the rest of the organization.

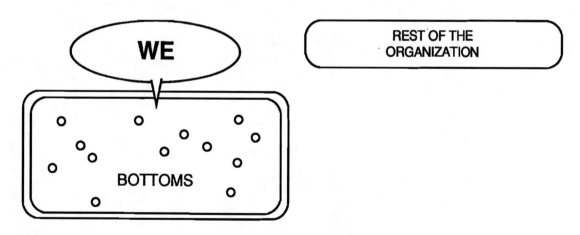

And Middles are diffused throughout the organization; they are "loners", not part of the Tops, or the Bottoms, and not connected to one another.

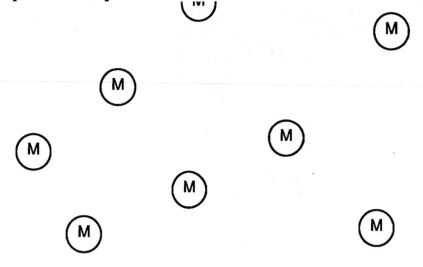

And outside the organization stand the Customers, looking to the organization for timely, quality, reasonably-priced products and services.

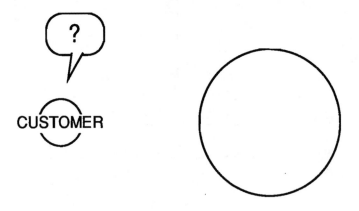

MEANWHILE ...

In this story, STRESS is everywhere.

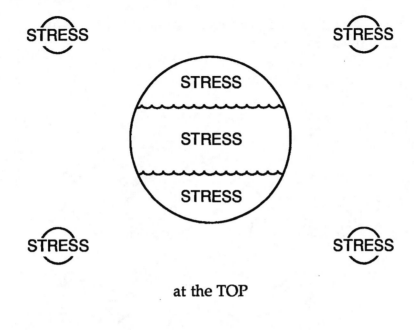

at the TOP

on the BOTTOM

in the MIDDLE

and among the CUSTOMERS.

Tops are overwhelmed by an unending stream of complications.

◊   There are complications coming in at them from the
     external environment;

◊   There are complications coming in at them from within the
     organization.

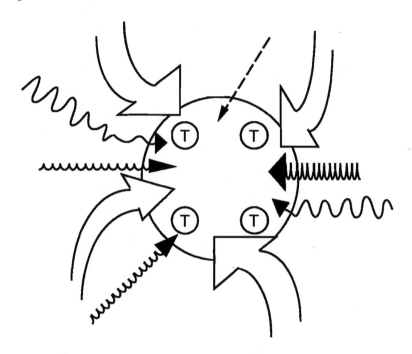

◊   There is too much to do and not enough time to do it;

◊   And Tops feel responsible for it all;

◊   And if there is any failure -- anywhere in the
     organization -- Tops take this as *their* personal failure.

Tops have lots of stress about this: pressure, urgency, high visibility, high
vulnerability.

Bottoms feel unseen and ignored.

MANAGEMENT

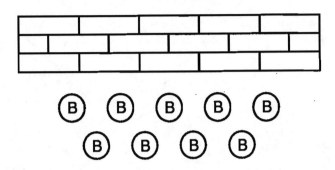

◊   Bottoms see many problems in the system.

    .. poor communication

    .. little direction

    .. conditions that shouldn't exist

    .. no inspiration, no big picture, no vision from above

    .. actions by Tops and Middles that make no sense

    .. unfair treatment.

◊   Bottoms feel that Tops and Middles *should* be handling these problems, and that they are not.

Bottoms have a lot of stress about this: frustration, resentment, anger, fear.

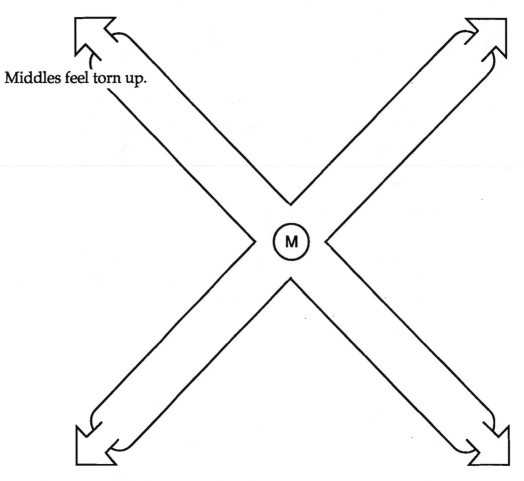

Middles feel torn up.

◊ They feel they *should* be able to deliver to Bottoms what Bottoms want but they don't get what they need from Tops to do that well.

◊ They feel they *should* be able to deliver to Tops what Tops want but they don't get the cooperation from Bottoms they need to do that well.

◊ And sometimes Tops and Bottoms want different and conflicting things from Middles.

Middles feel that they *should* be able to deliver for Tops;

that they *should* be able to deliver for Bottoms;

that they *should* be able to resolve the conflicts between Tops and Bottoms.

And Middles have lots of stress about that: feeling insufficient, inadequate, never quite measuring up to the job, never quite measuring up to what others want from them.

And there is stress among the Customers.

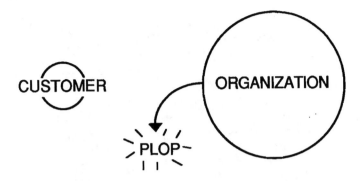

◊ Customers are not getting the products or services they
   want *when* they want them, to the *quality* they want them,
   or at the *price* they want them.

◊ Customers are puzzled; they can't understand why they are
   being treated this way.

◊ And Customers feel powerless to change that situation.

And Customers have lots of stress about that: frustration, anger, betrayal.

MEANWHILE . . .

There are problems in the relationships *among* peers:

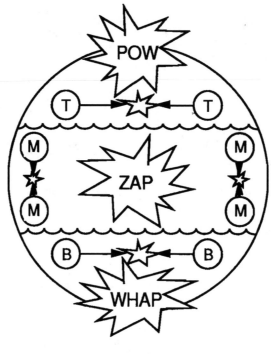

among TOPS

among BOTTOMS

and among MIDDLES.

Members of the Top team are engaged in territorial struggles with one another.

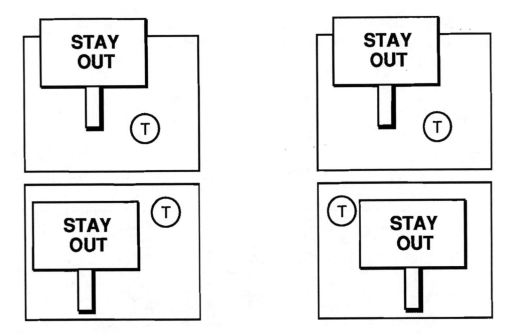

◊   Responsibilities are divided among Tops.

◊   Tops feel more responsible for their own turfs than for the organization as a whole.

◊   Things fall between the cracks, and Tops feel defensive and accusatory about whose responsibility that is.

◊   Tops feel the need to influence other Tops, and they feel shut out by them.

◊   Tops feel protective of their own turf; they resent and resist "incursions" by other Tops.

There is tension within Bottom groups.

There is a feeling of closeness and solidarity among Bottoms; and there is tension *among Bottoms* around maintaining that solidarity in the face of internal disagreement.

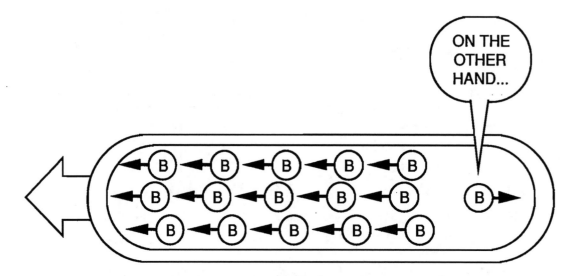

◊   Those who disagree with the majority feel vulnerable.

◊   And those in the majority feel threatened by disagreement.

◊   Disagreement is submerged.

And there is tension among the Middles.

There is no Middle group.

◊   Middles are "loners" in the organization.

◊   Not only are they separate from Tops and Bottoms, they are also isolated from one another.

◊   Each Middle experiences the pressures of the system alone, unsupported by other Middles.

◊   Middles are not drawn toward one another.

◊   They tend not to support one another,

◊   nor be supported by one another.

◊   They sometimes undermine and are undermined by one another,

◊   often unintentionally,

◊   and sometimes intentionally.

◊   They are often critical of one another.

◊   They generally feel they have little in common with one another.

◊   They have little interest in connecting with one another as peers.

◊   They see little potential power in connecting with other Middles, in supporting and being supported by one another.

MEANWHILE ...

Each part of the organization blocks or fails to support or cooperate with other parts of the organization.

Tops are not providing the vision, inspiration, direction, big picture that Middles and Bottoms look to them for.

Bottoms resist the frequent changes, re-arrangements, and re-directions Tops and Middles feel they *need* to make in order to cope with the complex and changing world.

Middles are not coming through strongly enough for either Tops or Bottoms; they are not providing the direction and support both look to them for.

Others in the organization see Tops as

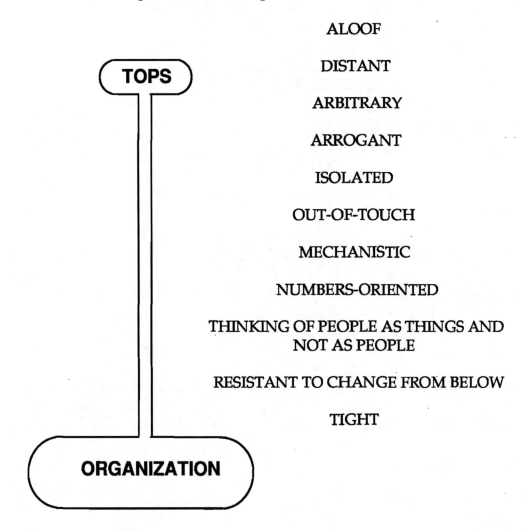

ALOOF

DISTANT

ARBITRARY

ARROGANT

ISOLATED

OUT-OF-TOUCH

MECHANISTIC

NUMBERS-ORIENTED

THINKING OF PEOPLE AS THINGS AND
NOT AS PEOPLE

RESISTANT TO CHANGE FROM BELOW

TIGHT

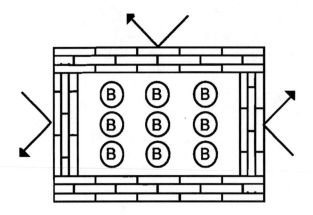

Others see Bottoms as

INFLEXIBLE

RESISTANT TO INFLUENCE

UNWILLING OR UNABLE TO ADAPT TO
RAPIDLY CHANGING CONDITIONS

And, depending on which way their *internal* conflicts are resolved...
Bottoms are seen either as

◊ LOYAL

◊ HARD-WORKING

◊ CREATIVE   *or as*

◊ TRUSTING

and as

◊ NAIVE and

◊ SCREWABLE

◊ SELFISH

◊ UNCONCERNED FOR
THE WELFARE OF THE
ORGANIZATION

◊ DEMANDING

◊ IMPATIENT

◊ RESISTING

◊ UNREASONABLE

and sometimes as

LISTLESS

APATHETIC

WEAK

DEAD

{M} {M} {M}

{M}

And others see Middles as

HARD-WORKING

RESPONSIBLE

{M}

WELL-INTENTIONED

{M}

and as

{M}

WEAK

{M}

WISHY-WASHY

NO MIND OF THEIR OWN

CONFUSED

{M}

POWERLESS

DON'T DELIVER

{M}

UNINFORMED

INCOMPETENT

FRACTIONATED

{M} {M}

{M}

People in each part of the organization feel they are not respected by people in other parts of the organization.

People throughout the organization feel misunderstood and unappreciated.

People in each part of the organization see people in other parts of the organization as acting toward them in ways that demonstrate MALICE, INSENSITIVITY, or INCOMPETENCE.

And each acts accordingly toward the others:

◊ attacking

◊ demanding

◊ withholding

◊ avoiding

◊ withdrawing.

And all feel justified in what they do.

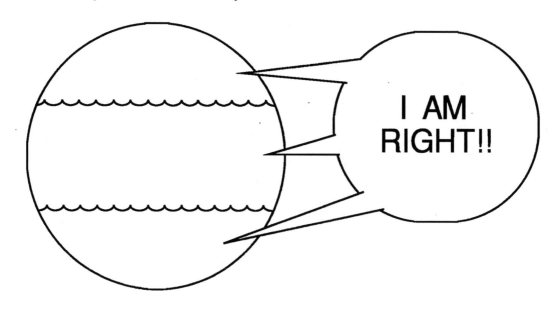

And the War continues...

as the organization struggles to survive in its complex and changing environment.

There are three possibilities in organizational life.

Of the three, INTERNAL WARFARE is the most costly.

It is also the easiest to play.

INTERNAL WARFARE happens without planning or thought.

Just put us together and say: Be an organization,

and INTERNAL WARFARE will quickly follow.

POSSIBILITY II:

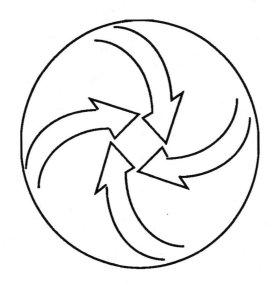

MAKING THINGS HAPPEN THROUGH MUTUAL UNDERSTANDING AND ACCOMMODATION

◊ How Warfare Develops

◊ Understanding and Accommodating to the Worlds of Tops, Bottoms, Middles, and Customers.

◊ Working The Center Ring or The Side Show

HOW WARFARE DEVELOPS

This is how INTERNAL WARFARE develops:

Here we are,

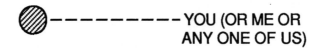

and then there are other people.

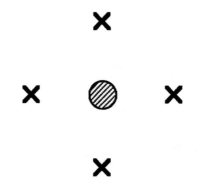

And it is as if these other people are behind walls.

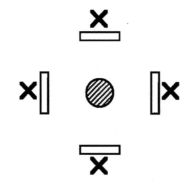

We don't really know what they do behind those walls,

and we don't know what life is like for them behind those walls.

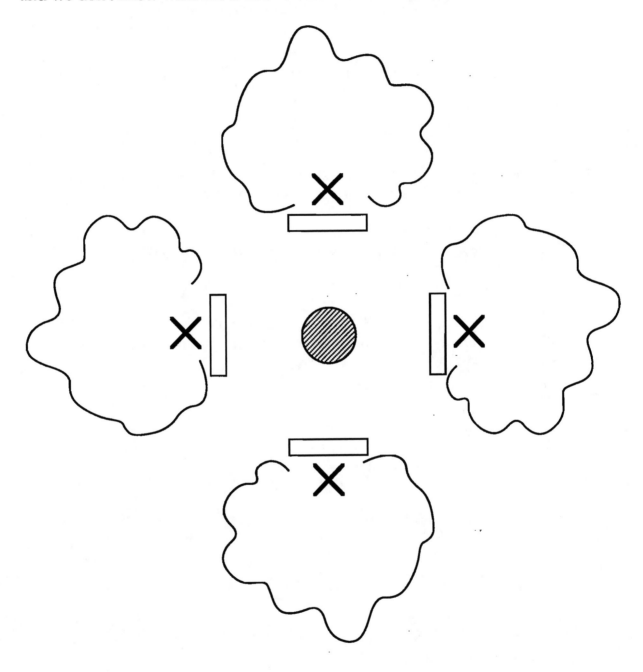

Still, "stuff" comes at us from these other people, from behind
their walls.

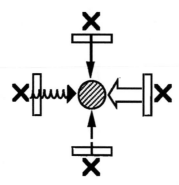

"Stuff" may be an order or a request or an announcement or a change in
previously given orders or requests or announcements.

"Stuff" may be how a person acts toward us: friendly or gruffly or ignoring us
completely.

And sometimes "stuff" is NOTHING. Nothing comes at us from behind a
wall, and we are looking to that wall for something: direction, guidance,
vision, inspiration.

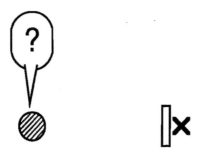

Sometimes this "stuff" makes no sense to us. It seems silly or stupid. It's a mystery.

What's going on behind that wall? What could they be thinking of?

In the absence of knowing, what we usually do is ...

make something up.

We make up a story that explains the "stuff".

We make up a story of who those people are and why they are doing what they are doing.

And when the "stuff" makes no sense to us, the story we make up is that the people behind the wall must be either

IGNORANT

MALICIOUS

INSENSITIVE

or

INCOMPETENT.

Why else would they be doing what they are doing?

And so we act accordingly; we

♢ attack

♢ demand

♢ withhold

♢ avoid

♢ withdraw.

And that becomes our "stuff" for them;

And they react accordingly,

And in no time, we are all seeing one another as ignorant, malicious, insensitive, and incompetent people.

And the war is on.

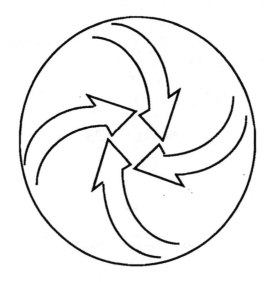

Tops, Middles, Bottoms and Customers

live behind their walls and in their worlds.

Each lives in a world very different from the other;

and each fails to see into the world of the others.

It is out of this condition that misunderstanding and warfare

develop.

So the challenge is this:

◊ Can we see into one another's worlds?

◊ Can we understand what life is really like for Tops,
   Middles, Bottoms and Customers?

◊ Can we use that understanding to avoid warfare

◊ and to make happen what we want to have happen?

UNDERSTANDING AND ACCOMMODATING

TO THE WORLD OF TOPS

The world of Tops is a world of COMPLICATIONS.

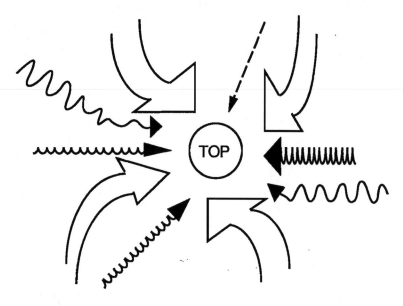

◊ It is a world of too much to do and not enough time to do it;

◊ there is an unending flow of matters to be handled

◊ issues to look at

◊ problems to solve

◊ inputs coming at you from outside the organization, from

consumers

the community

the government

competitors

new technology

◊ inputs coming at you from within the organization

◊ conflicting inputs, pulling you toward different directions

◊ complex problems

◊ difficult issues that haven't been handled elsewhere in the organization

◊ chronic problems that don't clear up

◊ new issues

◊ unpredictable issues.

And you feel responsible for handling it all.

And, in turbulent times,

when there are many demands on the organization

to adapt to changing conditions,

the world of Tops becomes more complicating.

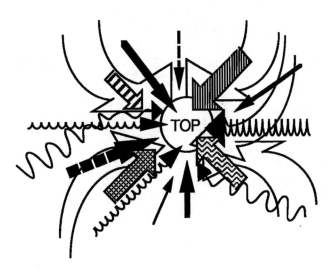

And many of the things that Tops do

are survival responses

in a world of complications --

protecting themselves against complications,

avoiding complications,

simplifying complications.

Sometimes the behavior of Tops seems strange to us;

sometimes we don't like what they do;

but, given the world of overloaded Tops, it all makes perfect sense:

It is the behavior of people reacting to, coping with, and

struggling to survive in a world of complications.

◊ Tops may create buffers between themselves and others as a way
   of protecting themselves against complexity.

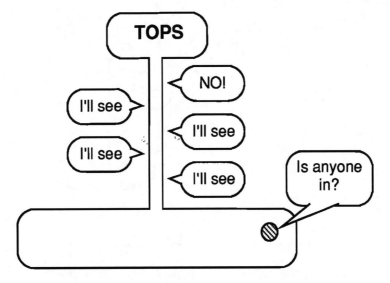

◊ And as a consequence, Tops become isolated, out of touch. And
   they continue to feel responsible for that with which they are
   out of touch.

◊ In their isolation Tops often become paranoid about what is
   going on "out there". The bad news floats up, but not the good.
   Tops envision plots and rebellions developing in the world
   they are isolated from.

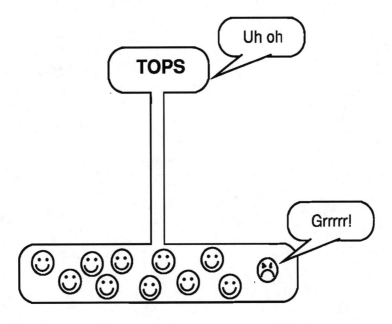

◊ In their isolation and out-of-touchness Tops take actions which are experienced by others as "off the wall". "Where did that come from?"

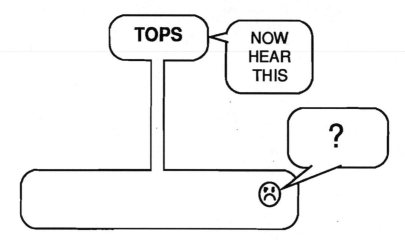

◊ And, what is most ironic, Tops may pass over opportunities in the environment. New possibilities, new business opportunities are experienced not as opportunities but as ... more complications.

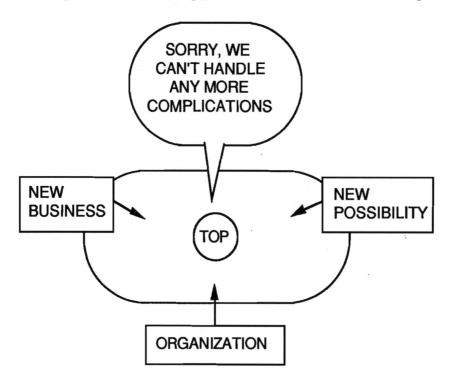

So,

when you enter the world of Tops, to do business with them,

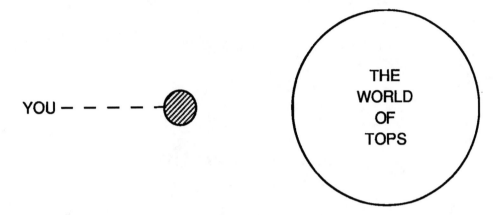

there is a good chance that you will be experienced as ...

MORE COMPLICATIONS.

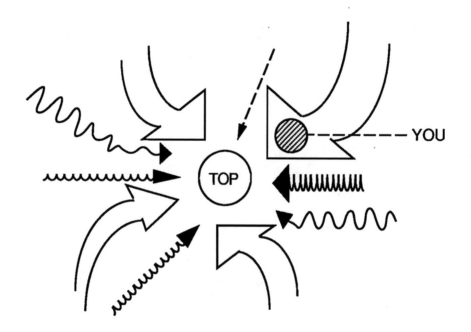

◊ You may be giving the Top a quality idea that could truly strengthen the organization;

◊ You may be proposing a structural change that would help the organization do better what it is supposed to do;

◊ You may be following up on an unanswered memo;

◊ You may be offering to provide feedback to a Top on what that Top did and how it could be done more effectively.

◊ You may be asking for direction and guidance.

◊ You may be offering to help in an area you know the Top wants help.

◊ You may be calling to have a friendly chat.

◊ You may have a great new possibility for the organization; a chance to move it into an unexplored and high potential area;

◊ You may be telling the Top what that Top needs to do in order not to lose some business;

◊ You may be offering the Top the opportunity for a big new piece of business.

From your perspective,

your proposals, recommendations, requests and actions

may be

simple

straightforward

logical

and reasonable.

But, to a Top, all of this may be experienced as ...

MORE COMPLICATIONS.

IT MEANS 50 %
MORE BUSINESS. . .
AN 80 % INCREASE
IN PROFITS . . . AN
OPPORTUNITY YOUR
PEOPLE CAN SINK
THEIR TEETH INTO . . .

WHO'S GOT
TIME
FOR
THIS?

TOP

So, in dealing with a Top,

beware:

You are not simply talking PERSON-TO-PERSON;

You are talking into a particular world, with particular characteristics;

You are talking into a world of COMPLICATIONS,

and there is every possibility

that what you are doing --

regardless of your intention --

will be experienced by a Top as

MORE COMPLICATIONS.

That may be how you will always show up for harassed Tops --

at first --

as more COMPLICATIONS.

The challenge is to accept that fact

and move beyond it.

The challenge is

      ◊ to be sensitive to the world of Tops

      ◊ to accommodate to that world

      ◊ to not add to Tops' complications

      ◊ to do what you can to decrease their complications.

The challenge is

      ◊ to support Tops in their world

      ◊ to get behind them

      ◊ to move them ahead.

While at the same time

      ◊ staying focused on your business

      ◊ on what you need Tops to do in order to move you ahead in your work.

UNDERSTANDING AND ACCOMMODATING

TO THE WORLD OF BOTTOMS

The world of Bottoms is a world of VULNERABILITY.

"THEM"

BOTTOM

"WE"

◊ It is a world in which you feel you need to protect yourself
  against "Them".

◊ It is a world in which "They" do stuff to you.

◊ It is a world in which you are on the receiving end of
  decisions affecting your life.

◊ It is a world in which you feel invisible to "Them" and they
  have power over you.

◊ It is a world in which things just happen to you –
  out of the blue, without your prior knowledge, involvement, or
  consent.

◊ It is a world of "We" versus "Them"
  and anyone who is not part of "We" is potentially part of "Them".

◊ It is a world in which you feel that in times of crisis
  "They" will take care of one another but not of you.

◊ It is a world in which you feel that "They" are out to get the most out of you at the least cost.

And, in turbulent times,

when there are many demands on the organization

to adapt to changing conditions,

the intensity of that vulnerability increases.

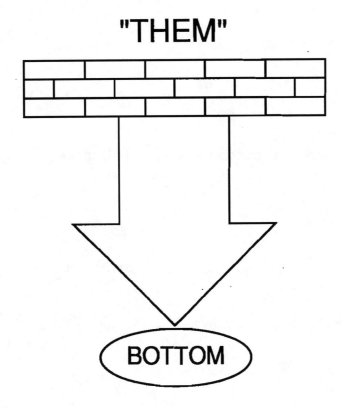

And many of the things that Bottoms do

are survival responses

in a world of vulnerability --

making themselves more secure in the system,

protecting themselves against being

tricked, abused, or taken advantage of by "Them".

Sometimes the behavior of Bottoms seems strange to us;

sometimes we don't like what they do;

but, given the world of vulnerable Bottoms, it all makes

perfect sense:

It is the behavior of people reacting to, coping with, and

struggling to survive in a world in which they feel vulnerable.

Some Bottoms cope with their vulnerability by becoming *good soldiers*, super-workers, pouring their energies into doing the work of the system. They struggle to become valued resources in the system. Resources that *will* be recognized, and safe.

Some Bottoms cope with vulnerability by becoming *victims* in the system. They experience the system -- other people, procedures -- as preventing them from producing the way they would like to produce. They complain about the system and how disruptive and non-supportive it is. They maintain that they *would* produce if only others didn't make it so difficult or impossible.

Some Bottoms immerse themselves in their work, existing as if they are *not* vulnerable when in fact they are.

Some Bottoms cope with vulnerability by leaving the system.

Some Bottoms cope with vulnerability by organizing, by developing collective power.

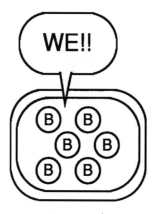

And some Bottoms cope with vulnerability in the system by withholding themselves from the system, by not caring about it, by staying emotionally distant from it.

So,

when you enter the world of Bottoms, to do business with them,

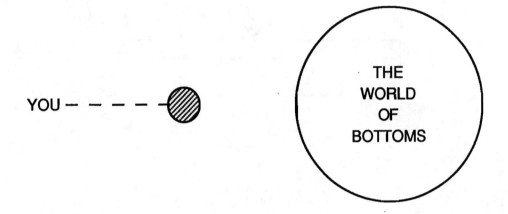

there is a good chance that you will be experienced ...

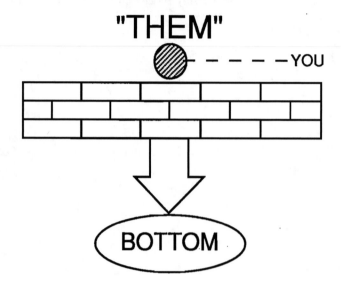

... as THEM

... as more danger to be protected
against.

◊ You may just be trying to do your job;

◊ You may be attempting to create a more democratic workplace;

◊ You may be introducing changes that will enhance the competitiveness and survivability of the organization;

◊ You may be helping Bottoms feel more a part of the organization;

◊ You may simply be passing down what your boss told you to do;

◊ You may be reorganizing work units to create more compatible and more effective work teams;

◊ You may be introducing new, more up-to-date, less cumbersome technology;

◊ You may be asking Bottoms for their opinions on how to improve the way work is done;

◊ You may be offering a training program aimed at developing new skills;

◊ You may be working on improving the quality of work life;

◊ You may be conducting a team development activity for work groups.

From your perspective,

your actions

may be

simple

straightforward

logical

and reasonable.

But, to a Bottom, all of this may be seen as ...

MORE VULNERABILITY

as "Them" trying to do it to us.

WHAT I'VE GOT FOR YOU IS
A GREAT NEW TECHNOLOGY . . .
EASY WORK . . . MORE CONTROL
OVER THE WORK FLOW . . .
A NEATER ENVIRONMENT . . .
MORE SAY IN WHAT HAPPENS
AROUND HERE . . . POWER . . .
GROWTH . . . SELF EXPRESSION
. . . DIGNITY . . .

THE WAY I HEAR IT
IS THIS: A JOB A
MONKEY CAN DO . . . A
50 % CUTBACK IN
THE WORKFORCE
WITHIN SIX MONTHS . . .
AN EVENTUAL
RELOCATION TO
PAGO PAGO . . .

BOTTOM

So, in dealing with Bottoms

beware:

You are not simply talking PERSON-TO-PERSON;

You are talking into a particular world

with particular characteristics;

You are talking into a world of VULNERABILITY;

and there is every possibility

that what you are doing --

regardless of your intention --

will be experienced by Bottoms

as a danger

as MORE VULNERABILITY.

That may be how you will always show up for vulnerable Bottoms...

at first ...

as more VULNERABILITY.

The challenge is to accept that fact

and move beyond it.

The challenge is

     ◊   to be sensitive to the world of Bottoms

     ◊   to accommodate to that world

     ◊   to not add to Bottoms' vulnerability in the system

     ◊   to do what you can to decrease that vulnerability.

The challenge is

     ◊   to support Bottoms in their world

     ◊   to get behind them

     ◊   to move them ahead.

While at the same time

     ◊   staying focused on your business

     ◊   on what you need Bottoms to do in order to move you ahead in your work.

UNDERSTANDING AND ACCOMMODATING

TO THE WORLD OF MIDDLES

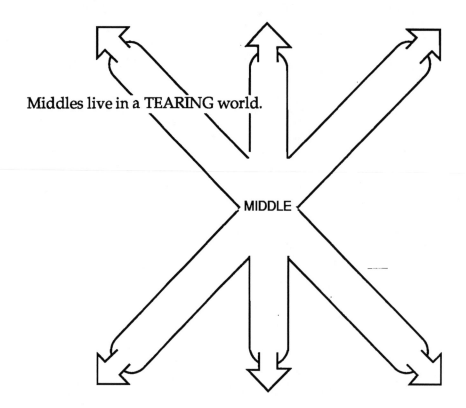

Middles live in a TEARING world.

MIDDLE

◊ It is a world in which people are pulling you in different directions;

◊ Tops have their priorities and they expect your support;

◊ Bottoms have their priorities -- which are generally different from Tops' -- and they expect your support;

◊ Tops want you to get production out of Bottoms

◊ but you can't do that without the cooperation of Bottoms;

◊ Bottoms want you to deliver on their needs and wants

◊ but often you can't do that without the cooperation of Tops.

◊ When Tops and Bottoms are in conflict, one or the other or both try to draw you in on their side.

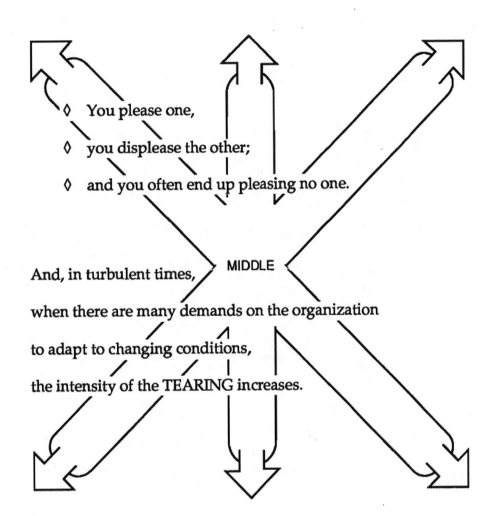

◊   You please one,

◊   you displease the other;

◊   and you often end up pleasing no one.

MIDDLE

And, in turbulent times,

when there are many demands on the organization

to adapt to changing conditions,

the intensity of the TEARING increases.

And many of the things that Middles do

are survival responses

in a tearing world --

    ◊   choosing sides so as not to be too torn,

    ◊   being fair to all sides so as to be equally torn,

    ◊   avoiding any side so as not to be torn at all.

Sometimes the behavior of Middles seems strange to us;

sometimes we don't like what they do;

but, given the world of torn Middles, it all makes perfect sense:

It is the behavior of people reacting to, coping with, and

struggling to survive in a tearing world.

Some Middles react to this tearing space by being fair. They try to be even-handed, unbiased. They try to please both sides.

◊ They work hard.

◊ They feel responsible for resolving conflicts.

◊ They never do enough to please either side.

◊ They get lots of negative feedback (or at the least, very little positive feedback).

◊ They are unsupported,

◊ under pressure.

◊ They begin to doubt themselves.

◊ Sometimes they just burn out trying to be fair.

HAS
ANYONE
SEEN
MIDDLE?

Some Middles cope with this tearing space by aligning themselves with Tops.

◊   They take the Top position.

◊   They become more top than the Tops.

◊   They are viewed by Bottoms as being unfair, untrustworthy, sellouts, weak, having no minds of their own.

Some Middles cope with the tearing space by aligning themselves with Bottoms.

◊   They take the Bottom position.

◊   They support Bottoms and protect them from the Tops.

◊   They are viewed by Tops (if they are viewed) as being weak, disloyal, not REAL management material.

Some Middles cope with the tearing space by bureaucratizing themselves, by putting protective walls around themselves, by making it so difficult to get to them that neither Tops nor Bottoms try very hard.

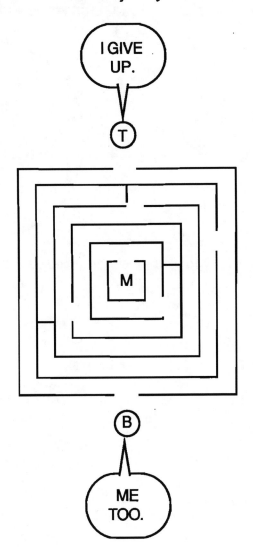

So,

when you enter the world of Middles, to do business with them

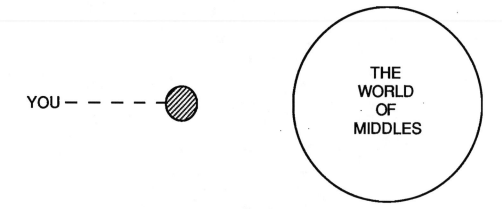

there is a good chance that you will be experienced as ...

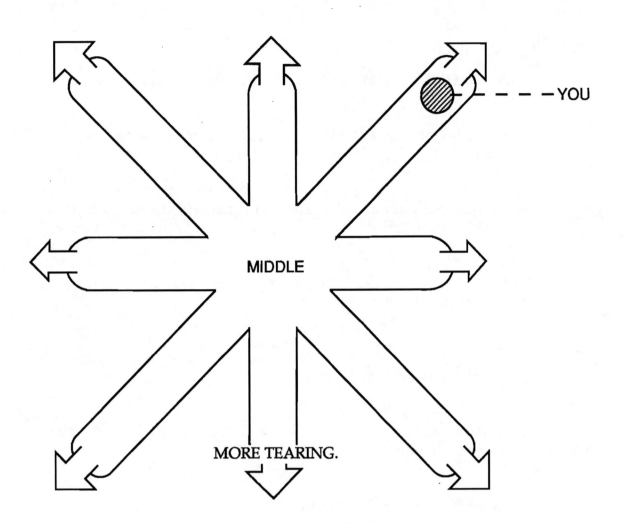

MIDDLE

MORE TEARING.

YOU

◊ As a Top you may ask a Middle to put some new work procedure into place;

◊ As a Bottom you may ask a Middle for materials you need;

◊ As a Top you may ask a Middle to gather some information you want;

◊ As a Bottom you may ask a Middle to change some unsatisfactory working conditions;

◊ As a Top you may ask a Middle to pass down and support some new policy direction;

◊ As a Bottom you may ask a Middle to pass up and support some complaint or grievance you have;

◊ As a Top you may expect and demand Middle support in the event of confrontation with Bottoms;

◊ As a Bottom you may expect and demand support from Middles in the event of "unfair" action on the part of Tops.

From your perspective --

as either a Top or Bottom --

your requests and demands

may be

simple

straightforward

logical

and reasonable.

But, to the Middle, all of these are experienced as ...

just more TEARING.

ALL I'M ASKING FOR IS A LOUSY 3 % INCREASE. WHAT KIND OF A BOSS CAN'T DELIVER ON A LOUSY 3 %?

LOOK, I DON'T CARE HOW GREAT THEY ARE . . . HOW HARD THEY'VE WORKED . . . WHAT YOU'VE PROMISED THEM. THERE IS NO MONEY. NONE. READ MY LIPS. NONE!

HELP!!

MIDDLE

And if a Middle doesn't react

as fast as you want

or as effectively as you want,

you increase the pressure

which, from your perspective,

seems like a reasonable thing to do.

And this ends up ...

increasing the tearing on Middle

from all sides.

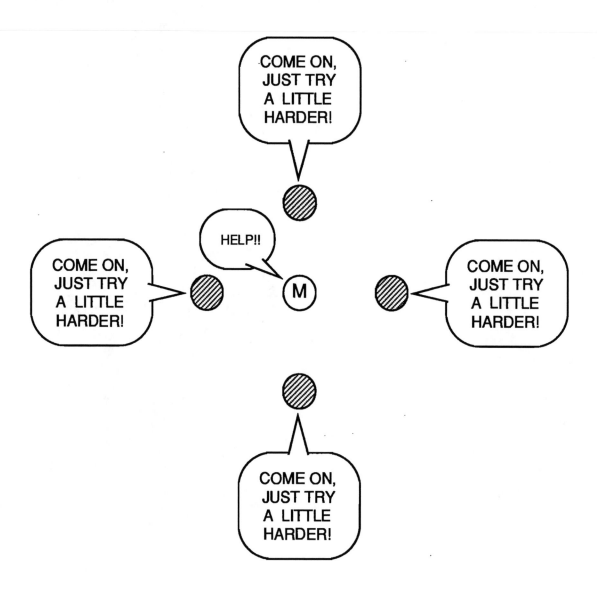

So, in dealing with Middles

beware:

You are not simply talking PERSON-TO-PERSON;

You are talking into a world with particular characteristics;

You are talking into a TEARING world,

and there is every possibility

that what you are doing --

regardless of your intention --

will be experienced by Middles

as MORE TEARING.

That may be how you will always show up for torn Middles ...

at first,

as more TEARING.

The challenge is to accept that fact

and move beyond it.

The challenge is

◊   to be sensitive to the world of Middles

◊   to accommodate to that world

◊   to not increase the tearing on Middles

◊   to do what you can to decrease that tearing.

The challenge is

◊   to support Middles in their world

◊   to get behind them

◊   to move them ahead.

While at the same time

◊   staying focused on your business

◊   on what you need Middles to do in order to move you ahead in your work.

UNDERSTANDING AND ACCOMMODATING

TO THE WORLD OF CUSTOMERS

The world of Customers is a world of Neglect.

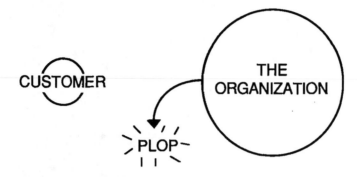

◊ It is a world of disappointment --

◊ products or services not delivered

◊ or not delivered

when you want them

to the quality you want them

at the price you want them.

◊ It is a world of promises made

◊ and promises broken.

◊ It is a world in which you as a Customer are too small

to have impact on that BIG organization.

◊   It is a world in which your feedback (your complaints and suggestions)

disappear into a black hole.

◊   It is a world of always dealing with the wrong people

◊   and never with those people who can do anything about your problems.

And, in turbulent times,

when there are many demands on the organization

to adapt to changing conditions,

the intensity of that Neglect increases.

And many of the things that Customers do

are survival responses

in a world of Neglect --

coping with their frustration, anger and powerlessness.

Sometimes the behavior of Customers seems strange to us;

sometimes we do not like what they do;

but, given the world of neglected Customers, it all makes

perfect sense:

It is the behavior of people reacting to, coping with, and

struggling to survive in a world of Neglect.

Some Customers express their outrage to the organization.
Sometimes this yields results, and sometimes it makes it easy for the
organization not to provide service to such "difficult" and "unpleasant"
persons.

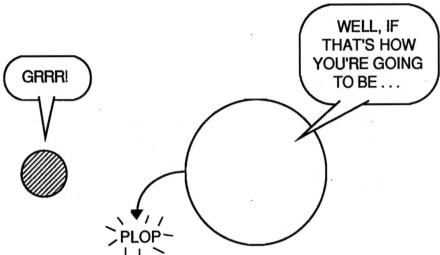

Some Customers react with patience and trust, and their frustration and
anxiety mount as the organization continues to offer low quality service.

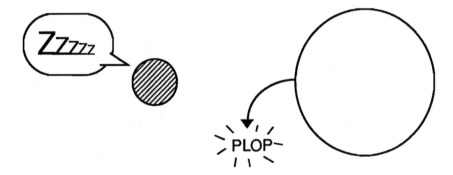

Some Customers adjust their standards to what the organization seems able
to produce. They come to expect less. They are satisfied with less.

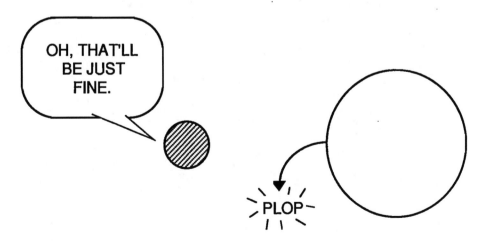

Some Customers leave to find other providers.

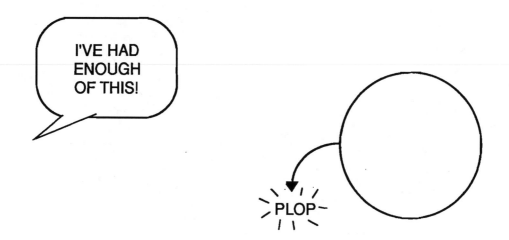

And some Customers find the same problems everywhere and slip into resignation. This is the way things are and the way they will be. There's no sense looking for or expecting anything else.

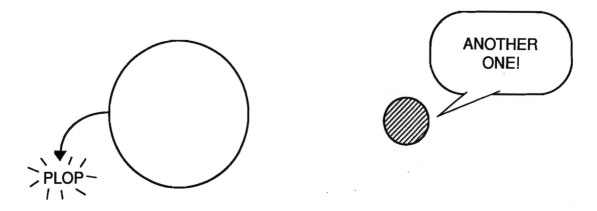

So,

when you enter the world of Customers, to do business with them,

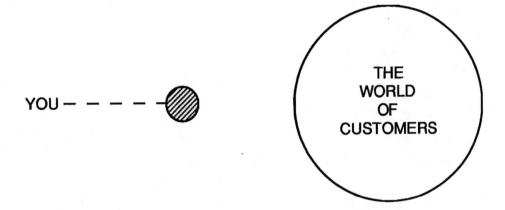

there is a good chance that you will be experienced as ...

MORE NEGLECT.

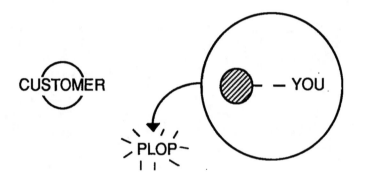

◊ You may be giving Customers the BIG PICTURE -- explaining to them the reasons for poor delivery;

◊ You may be apologizing to Customers for the poor delivery they are getting;

◊ You may be explaining to Customers what it is they need to do in order to get good delivery;

◊ You may be asking Customers to be patient, to wait, to give the system time to deliver;

◊ You may be making promises to Customers about future delivery;

◊ You may be asking Customers to give you the problem to work on,

◊ and to trust you to handle it well.

From your perspective,

your actions and requests

may be

simple

straightforward

logical

and reasonable.

But, to the Customer, all of this may be seen as ...

MORE NEGLECT.

RELAX . . . CALL THIS
NUMBER . . . MONDAY
AT NINE . . . ASK FOR
CHARLIE . . . GIVE HIM
MY NAME . . . **YOUR
PROBLEM IS SOLVED !**

SURE . . . THAT NUMBER
WON'T WORK . . .
CHARLIE WILL BE
SICK . . . NO ONE WILL
HAVE HEARD OF
YOU . . . AND **MONDAY
IS A HOLIDAY !**

YOU —

CUSTOMER

So, in dealing with Customers,

beware:

You are not simply talking PERSON-TO-PERSON;

You are talking into a particular world

with particular characteristics;

You are talking into a world of NEGLECT,

and there is every possibility

that what you are doing --

regardless of your intention --

will be experienced by a Customer

as MORE NEGLECT.

That may be how you will always show up for

Neglected Customers ...

at first ...

as more NEGLECT.

The challenge is

     ◊ to be sensitive to the world of Customers

     ◊ to accommodate to that world

     ◊ to not add to Customers' neglect

     ◊ to do what you can to decrease that neglect.

The challenge is

     ◊ to support Customers in their world

     ◊ to get behind them

     ◊ to move them ahead.

While at the same time

     ◊ staying focused on your business

     ◊ on what you need Customers to do in order to move you ahead in your work.

So...

Tops

Middles

Bottoms and

Customers live in different worlds,

And the same item --

an event

an idea

a suggestion

a rumor

an interaction --

may show up very differently in each of their worlds.

TAKE THIS BOOK FOR EXAMPLE.

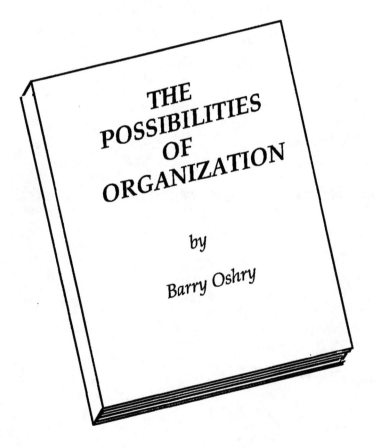

My purpose in writing this book

is to open up productive possibilities for

Tops

Bottoms

Middles

and Customers --

CLARITY AND EMPOWERMENT.

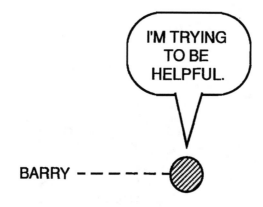

But that may not be how the book shows up

in the worlds

of Tops

Bottoms

Middles

and Customers.

To Tops,

already overwhelmed by feelings of responsibility and complications,

the book may show up as a personal attack on them

and as more COMPLICATIONS.

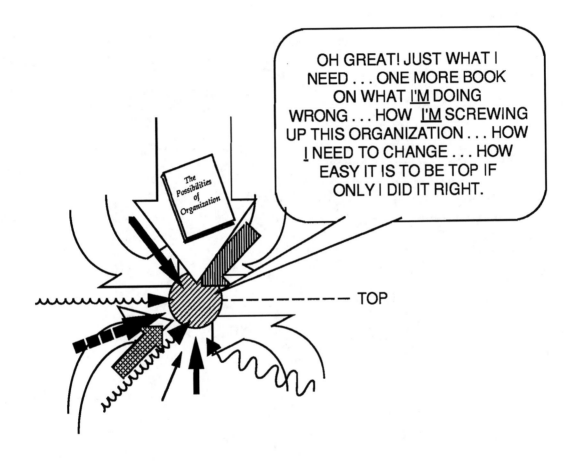

To Bottoms,

already feeling vulnerable in the system,

the book may show up as more danger.

I show up as "Them" doing it to us again, as creating

more vulnerability.

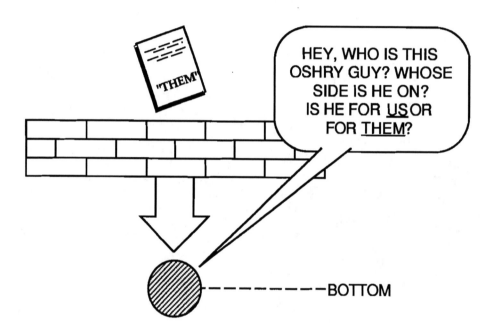

To Middles,

feeling torn up between others in the system,

the book may show up as something that alleviates that tearing.

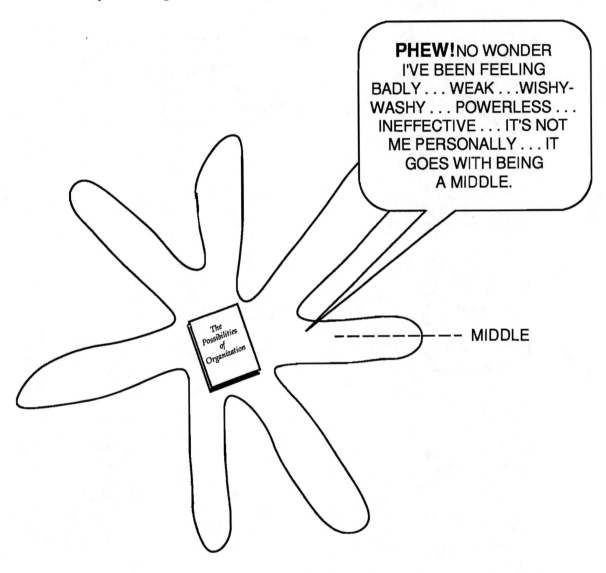

And to Customers

who are feeling neglected,

the book may show up as more neglect.

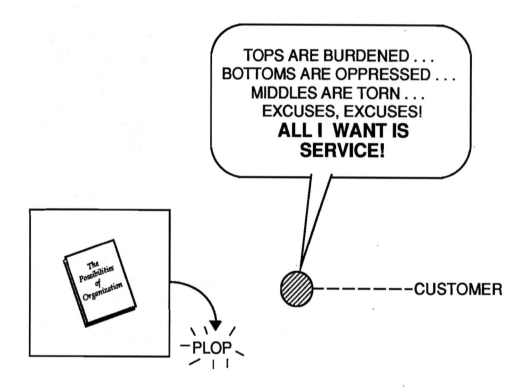

Or take the possibility of partnership in the organization.

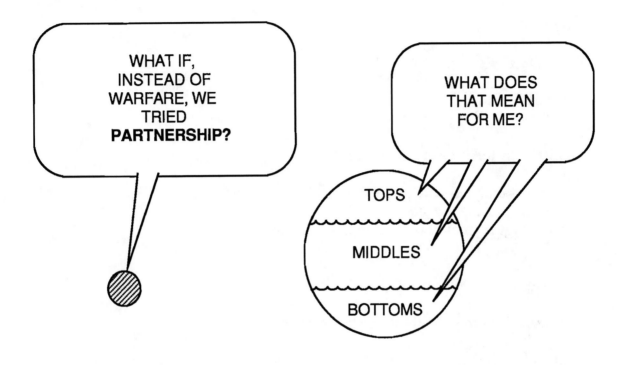

Working in partnership with one another may offer productive

possibilities for

TOPS,

BOTTOMS,

and MIDDLES:

Possibilities for greater accomplishment,

for more satisfying and more productive relationships,

and for higher quality service to the Customer.

But, how does the possibility of partnership

show up in each of their worlds?

To TOPS, who feel responsibility for everything

in the organization,

the possibility of partnership may be experienced as dangerous.

    ◊ It raises questions of trust. Can I trust them to be
      responsible for what in the final analysis I remain
      responsible for?

    ◊ It raises questions of control. Will I be able to
      influence what they do?

MORE COMPLICATIONS!
AM I GOING TO LOSE
CONTROL? . . . CAN I TRUST
THEM? . . . WHAT'S WRONG
WITH HOW I'VE BEEN
DOING THINGS?

-------TOP

To BOTTOMS, the possibility of partnership may be experienced

as "THEM" unloading their responsibilities on "Us",

as "THEM" trying to get more work out of us.

WHAT ARE THEY UP
TO NOW? . . . IS THIS
A NEW TRICK? . . . MORE
WORK, SAME MONEY . . .
WHAT HAPPENED TO
LAST YEAR'S GREAT IDEA?

- - - - - - -BOTTOM

To MIDDLES, the possibility of partnership may at first

promise relief;

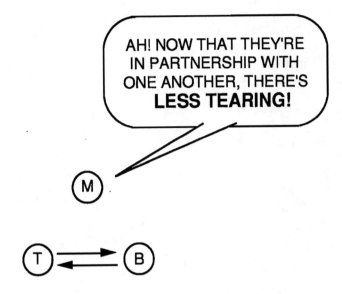

and, in time, it may pose new dilemmas.

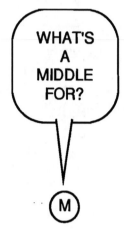

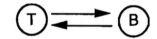

It is an endless challenge for us to recognize the

different worlds around us

and to speak appropriately into these different worlds.

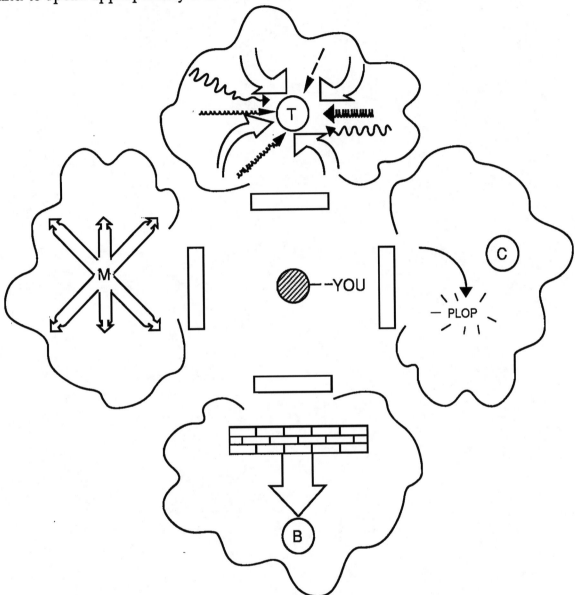

Much of the time

we speak to others out of what makes sense in our world

and not in theirs;

and then we wonder why we are so misunderstood.

THE CENTER RING

AND

THE SIDE SHOWS

In the organization we are potentially in the center of the

Center Ring.

We deal with Tops, with Middles, with Bottoms, with Customers.

Our business is to interact with these folks in ways that make

it possible -- even easy -- for them to do what we need them to

do in order for us to move ahead in our work.

[That is so important, let's say it again.]

IN THE CENTER RING,

OUR BUSINESS IS TO INTERACT

WITH PEOPLE

IN WAYS THAT MAKE IT POSSIBLE --

EVEN EASY --

FOR THEM TO DO

WHAT WE NEED THEM TO DO

IN ORDER FOR US

TO MOVE AHEAD IN OUR WORK.

In the Center Ring,

our business is to stay focused on that --

making happen what we want to have happen,

making happen what the system needs to have happen --

having empathy and understanding for other people and their efforts to survive in their worlds,

being strategic,

taking their worlds into account,

not being distracted,

not getting hooked by the "stuff" that comes at us from over the wall,

not making it hard for people to do what we need them to do,

not making it easy for them not to do what we need them to do.

Which brings us to THE SIDE SHOWS.

MUCH OF WHAT TAKES PLACE IN ORGANIZATIONAL LIFE

TAKES PLACE NOT IN THE CENTER RING

BUT IN THE SIDE SHOWS.

There we are, out in the world, trying to make happen

what we want to have happen

and what the system needs to have happen.

Our goals are clear,

our intentions noble.

We are interacting with Tops,

with Middles,

with Bottoms and

with Customers.

And then...

"STUFF" HAPPENS!

◊ A Top does not answer two phone calls.

◊ A Bottom grunts and walks away when we suggest a work change.

◊ A Customer angrily threatens to take her business away when she learns about a slight delay in delivery.

◊ A Middle changes his mind.

◊ A Top ignores us when we greet her in the corridor.

◊ A Middle fails to deliver on a promise.

◊ A Bottom complains about how little we do and questions what we get paid for.

◊ We get an argument when we expected agreement.

◊ We get glazed eyes when we expected enthusiasm.

This and other "stuff" comes at us from behind the walls.

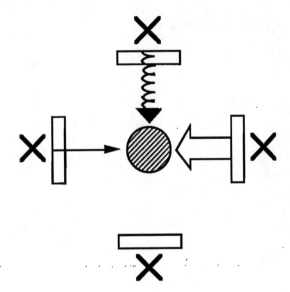

And the Side Show begins when we get hooked on dealing with

the "stuff" and we are no longer focused on interacting with folks in

a way that makes it possible -- even easy -- for them to do what

we need them to do.

In the Side Show what matters to us is what others did to us

and the meaning we attribute to their actions. They have

>snubbed us

>or attacked us

>or insulted us

>or belittled us

>or ignored us.

They have done this because they are

>malicious

>or ignorant

>or insensitive

>or incompetent.

Or because we are

> insignificant
>
> unworthy
>
> losers
>
> threats to them
>
> or incompetent.

And we react by

> retaliating
>
> or undermining them
>
> or smoldering inside
>
> or getting depressed
>
> or plotting revenge
>
> or looking for another job.

The Side Shows are rich and dramatic times for us.

They provide material for dynamic conversations over water coolers, in restrooms, dining rooms, bars, and over kitchen tables.

They add drama to our lives in the organization: the battles we are in and the odds we must overcome.

The Side Shows have everything ... almost.

They have:

> good guys and bad guys
>
> crises
>
> suspense
>
> successs
>
> and failure.

They offer us something we cannot get in the Center Ring.

They offer us drama,

the opportunity to play a part

in which we are the

> righteous,
>
> virtuous,
>
> helpless,
>
> blameless,
>
> victims of others.

Such parts are not available to us in the Center Ring.

In the Center Ring:

◊ our business is to make happen what we want to have
happen and what the system needs to have happen,

◊ our business is to interact with others in ways that make
it possible -- even easy -- for them to do what we need them to do in
order to move ahead with our work.

That business cannot happen so long as we are hooked by other

people's "stuff".

In organizational life, "stuff" will continue to come at us from over the walls

of Tops, Middles, Bottoms, and Customers.

Nothing is going to stop that "stuff" from coming.

So the question is: How do we experience that "stuff"?

Do we see it as the intentional actions of people who are malicious or

ignorant or insensitive or incompetent?

Do we take it as personal attacks on us?

Or do we see it as the consequence of people struggling to survive in the face

of the unique conditions of their environments?

Do we get hooked on that "stuff"?

Or do we move past it?

SUMMARY

MUTUAL UNDERSTANDING and ACCOMMODATION is the second possibility of organization.

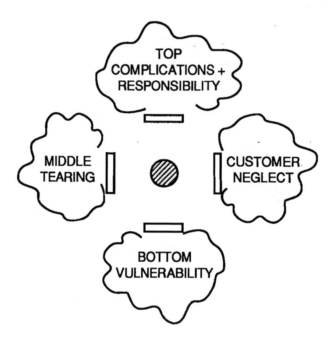

◊ We can attempt to see into, comprehend, accept and adjust to one another's worlds;

◊ We can accommodate to others, acting in ways that make it possible, easy even, for them to do what we need them to do in order for us to move ahead with our work;

◊ We can see the "stuff" that comes at us from others as the behavior of people struggling to cope with and survive in the unique conditions of their worlds;

◊ We can choose NOT to get hooked on that stuff.

ACCOMMODATION is about them -- about those Tops, those Bottoms, those Middles and those Customers, and about what we need to do to interact more effectively with them.

TRANSFORMATION, the third possibility, is about us -- and about the possibility of transforming organizations by transforming the way we play our roles as Tops, Bottoms, Middles, and Customers.

POSSIBILITY III:

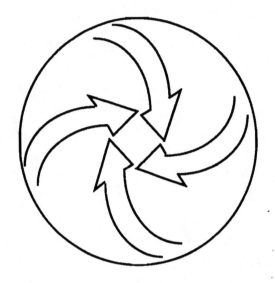

TRANSFORMATION

Transforming organizations by transforming the

way we play our parts as Tops, Middles, Bottoms,

and Customers.

◊ How We Fall Into Becoming Burdened Tops,
  Torn Middles, Oppressed Bottoms, and
  Screwed Customers.

◊ Why Change Doesn't Happen.

◊ What Else is Possible? Creating More Powerful
  Strategies for Ourselves as Tops, Middles, Bottoms,
  and Customers.

TOPS FEEL BURDENED BY RESPONSIBILITY AND COMPLEXITY

BOTTOMS FEEL OPPRESSED BY "THEM"

MIDDLES FEEL TORN UP

AND CUSTOMERS FEEL SCREWED BY DELIVERY SYSTEMS THAT
DON'T DELIVER

This is the story that occurs with great regularity.

It is a disempowering story;

it disempowers us,

it disempowers our relationships with others,

it disempowers our organizations.

It is a predictable story

but not an inevitable one.

It is a story we fall into.

And this is how we fall.

There are certain common conditions that occur again and again

in organization life.

These conditions go with what it is to be in an organization.

$$\boxed{\begin{array}{c}\textbf{COMMON}\\\textbf{CONDITIONS}\end{array}}$$

These conditions are not likely to disappear. So long as there
are organizations these conditions will be around.

There are certain predictable responses we make to these
conditions.

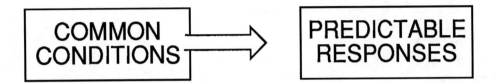

These responses are so basic to us that they are not experienced as choices.

They are the way we as human beings respond to these conditions --
instinctively, without thought or choice.

Create the conditions, and you can count on us -- for the most
part -- to respond in these predictable ways.

And once we make these predictable responses we fall into certain realities. The realities we fall into are the familiar realities of organizational life.

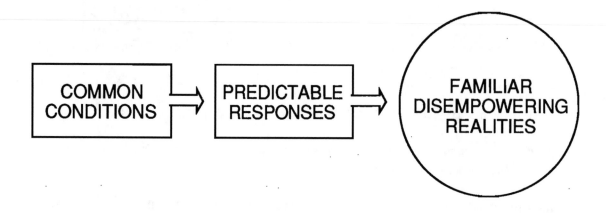

Here is how Tops, Middles, Bottoms and Customers fall into their familiar realities...

TOPS

FALLING INTO BURDEN

Top Overload is a common condition in the Top position

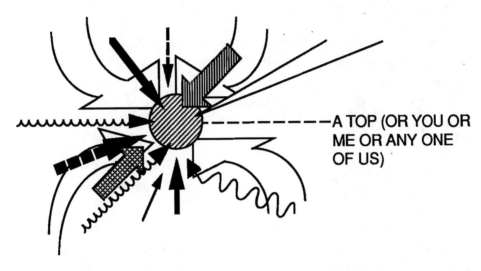

A TOP (OR YOU OR ME OR ANY ONE OF US)

but it is not limited to that position.

We are in Top Overload whenever we are responsible for some whole operation (the total organization or our piece of it, or a project team, or a task force, or a classroom, etc.)

and the situation we are responsible for is very complex.

TOP
OVERLOAD

OUR PREDICTABLE RESPONSE WHEN WE ARE IN TOP OVERLOAD IS
TO SUCK UP ALL RESPONSIBILITY TO OURSELVES AND AWAY FROM
OTHERS.

◊ We don't think about sucking up responsibility, it just happens.

◊ It's not like making a choice, we simply do it.

◊ It is like a hook we swallow.

◊ As human beings, this is how we respond to Top Overload   -- not all
   of us, not every time, but with great regularity.

◊ Create the condition of Top Overload, and we respond --
   without thought -- by sucking up all responsibility to
   ourselves.

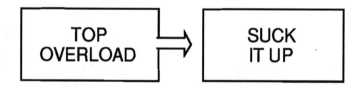

And in reacting this way, we unknowingly fall into a certain

reality about what it is to be a Top.

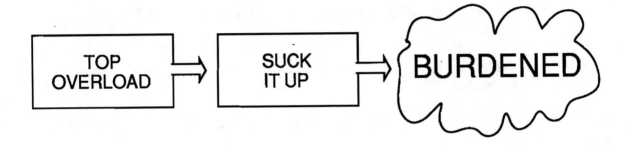

It is a familiar Top reality.

◊ It is a world in which we are burdened by what feel to be unmanageable complications.

◊ It is a world in which we feel largely alone and unsupported in our responsibility.

◊ We worry about all the things we should be doing but are not doing.

◊ We worry about the things we are doing...but not doing well enough.

◊ We worry about our ever-growing agenda.

◊ Many people are depending on us; and we fear we are letting them down.

◊ We fight fires; we deal with crises.

◊ We make decisions because someone must decide; but we aren't sure they are the right decisions.

◊ It is a world in which our options are limited to how we deal with burden -- work longer, work harder, continue the search for better support, resign.

This feels like reality.

It feels solid to us, like the way things are.

We are burdened; and it feels to us as if we are burdened because of circumstances-beyond-our-control.

Still, it is a reality we have fallen into, unaware that we have done so.

And once we fall, BURDEN is inevitable.

BOTTOMS

FALLING INTO OPPRESSION

Bottom Disregard is a common condition in the Bottom position

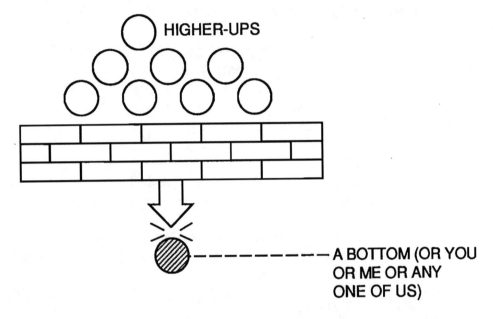

but it is not limited to that position. We are in Bottom Disregard whenever:

◊ we see negative conditions in the organization;

◊ some of these conditions affect us directly, and some are just things we see that are wrong with the organization;

◊ we believe that others -- "higher-ups" in the organization -- could fix these conditions if they chose to; and

◊ they don't.

BOTTOM
DISREGARD

OUR PREDICTABLE RESPONSE WHEN WE ARE IN THE CONDITION OF

BOTTOM DISREGARD IS TO HOLD THE "HIGHER-UPS" RESPONSIBLE

FOR WHAT'S WRONG.

We make it their business to fix whatever is wrong,

whether it's our situation or anything else in the organization.

    ◊ We don't think about giving "them" responsibility for
      us and the system, it just happens.

    ◊ It's not like making a choice, we simply do it.

    ◊ It is like a hook we swallow.

    ◊ As human beings this is how we respond to Bottom Disregard ...
      not all of us, not every time, but with great regularity.

    ◊ Create the condition of Bottom Disregard, and we respond -- without
      thought -- by holding higher-ups responsible for our condition and
      for the condition of the system.

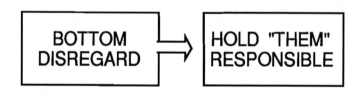

And in reacting that way, we unknowingly fall into a certain

reality about what it is to be a Bottom.

It is a familiar Bottom reality.

◊ It is a world in which our lives and the organization's life
  are in the hands of others -- higher-ups -- and they are making a
  mess of it.

◊ It is a world in which we are hooked on "them", what they are
  doing and not doing, and on our feelings towards them.

◊ We feel angry at them, disappointed in them, betrayed by them.

◊ We are oppressed (ignored, unrecognized, mistreated) by them;
  they are doing this to us.

◊ It is a world in which our options are limited to how we deal
  with oppression -- accept it as our lot, suffer in silence, complain,
  resist, rebel.

This is reality.

It feels solid to us, like the way things are. It is a reality

beyond our control.

Still, it is a reality we have fallen into, unaware that we have done so.

And once we fall, our experience of being OPPRESSED by "Them" is

inevitable.

MIDDLES

FALLING INTO TORN

Middle Crunch is a common condition in the middle position,

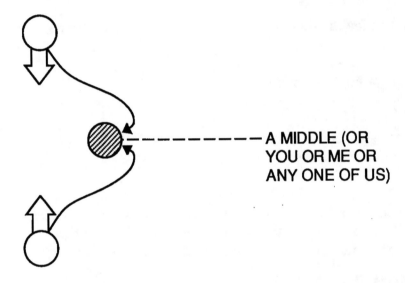

A MIDDLE (OR
YOU OR ME OR
ANY ONE OF US)

but it is not limited to that position. We are in Middle Crunch whenever:

◊ we exist between two or more people in the
organization who are in disagreement with one another

◊ or who have differing priorities or perspectives, and

◊ one or more parties is pulling us into the middle,
wanting us on their side, understanding them, sympathizing with
them, supporting them, working for them.

```
MIDDLE
CRUNCH
```

OUR PREDICTABLE RESPONSE WHEN WE ARE IN THE CONDITION OF MIDDLE CRUNCH IS TO SLIDE INTO THE MIDDLE OF OTHER PEOPLE'S ISSUES AND CONFLICTS AND MAKE THEIR ISSUES AND CONFLICTS OUR ISSUES AND CONFLICTS.

◊ We don't think about sliding into the middle; we just do it.

◊ It doesn't feel like a choice we make; it simply happens.

◊ It is like a hook we swallow.

◊ It is how we as human beings respond to Middle Crunch ... not all of us, not every time, but with great regularity.

◊ Create the condition of Middle Crunch and we respond -- without thought -- by sliding into the middle of conflicts between others such that their conflicts become ours.

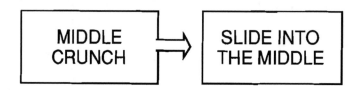

And, in reacting that way, we unknowingly fall into a certain reality about

what it is to be a Middle.

It is a familiar Middle reality.

◊ It is a world in which we are torn between others, pushed and pulled by them, reacting to them. It is a world in which both sides question our commitment to them, our loyalty to them.

◊ It is a world in which we lose our independence of thought and action. What matters is what they think and what they want. We, as independent thinkers and actors, disappear.

◊ It is a world in which we are feeling responsible for the problems between them; it is a world in which we are never doing enough.

◊ It is a world in which we feel confused, weak, uncertain -- in which we get little positive feedback from anyone,

◊ and in which, in time, we begin to question our own competence.

◊ It is a world in which our options are limited to surviving in an environment that threatens to tear us apart -- we can align ourselves with the Tops, or we can align ourselves with the Bottoms, or we can so thoroughly bureaucratize ourselves that no one can get at us, or we can try to be evenhanded to both sides and burn ourselves out in the process.

This tearing world feels like reality.

It feels solid to us, like the way things are.

It feels like a reality-beyond-our-control.

Still, it is a reality we have fallen into, unaware that we have done so.

And once we fall, our experience of being TORN is inevitable.

CUSTOMERS

FALLING INTO BEING SCREWED

Customer Neglect is a common condition among Customers of an organization

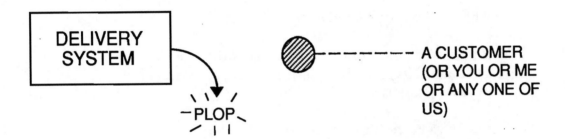

but it is not limited to Customers in that sense. This is a condition we are in whenever

◊ we are dependent on some provider (an organization or group or individual) to provide us with some product or service we want;

◊ and they don't provide it, or

◊ they don't provide it when we want it, at a cost we consider reasonable, or at a level of quality we consider acceptable.

OUR PREDICTABLE RESPONSE WHEN WE ARE IN THE CONDITION OF
CUSTOMER NEGLECT IS TO STAND ALOOF FROM THE DELIVERY
PROCESS (NOT GET MIXED UP IN IT), AND TO HOLD THE DELIVERY
SYSTEM RESPONSIBLE FOR DELIVERING THE PRODUCT OR SERVICE.

◊ We don't decide to stay aloof from the delivery process,
   it just happens.

◊ We don't choose to hold them responsible; we just do.

◊ It is like a hook we swallow.

◊ This is how we as human beings respond to the condition
   of Customer Neglect... not all of us, not every time, but
   with great regularity.

◊ Put us in the condition of Customer Neglect and we
   respond -- without thought -- by staying aloof from the
   delivery process, and by putting responsibility for delivery onto the
   delivery system.

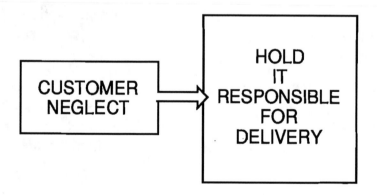

And, in reacting that way, we unknowingly fall into a certain reality about what it is to be a Customer.

It is a familiar Customer reality.

◊ It is a world in which we feel entitled -- we are the Customer; it is our right to be receiving quality products and services.

◊ It is a world of constant frustration and disappointment -- promises made, promises broken.

◊ It is a world in which we are the righteous, blameless victims of unresponsive delivery systems.

◊ It is a world in which our options are limited to the different ways we respond to being screwed -- suffer in silence, seek another delivery system, complain, settle for less than satisfactory delivery.

This world of being screwed feels like a reality to us.

It feels solid, like the way things are.

It feels like a reality beyond our control.

Still, it is a reality we have fallen into, unaware that we have done so.

And once we fall, our experience of being SCREWED by the organization is inevitable.

So, there is a story that happens with great regularity.

It is a story we fall into.

It is a story in which, as Tops, we fall into sucking up responsibility to ourselves, and then find ourselves living in a world of Burden.

It is a story in which, as Bottoms, we fall into giving over to higher-ups -- to "THEM" -- responsibility for our condition and for the condition of the organization, and then find ourselves living in a world in which "THEY" are making a mess out of our lives and the organization.

It is a story in which, as Middles, we fall into sliding into the middle of others' issues and conflicts -- losing our independent selves in their issues and conflicts -- and then find ourselves struggling to survive in a world that tears us apart.

It is a story in which, as Customers, we fall into turning over to delivery systems responsibility for delivering what we want, and then find ourselves living in a world in which we are the righteously screwed Customers of inadequately responsive systems.

We do all of this unaware that we are doing anything.

It feels to us that we are victims of these conditions, that they happen to us, that, as Tops, we are burdened because our world is burdensome.

As Bottoms, we are oppressed because they are oppressing us.

As Middles, we are torn because our job is a tearing job.

As Customers, we are screwed because the delivery system is screwing us.

All of this is experienced as reality -- as the way things really are.

We have no part in any of this.

That is how it seems.

WALL STREET JOURNAL

VOL. MMMDXVII   JAN. 2   3010

Recent Research Findings:

TOPS STILL SUCKING IT UP.
BOTTOMS STILL BLAMING "THEM."
MIDDLES STILL LOSING
THEMSELVES IN THE MIDDLE
CUSTOMERS STILL HOLDING
DELIVERY SYSTEMS
RESPONSIBLE FOR DELIVERY

FINDINGS UNCHANGED SINCE 1986, FIRST YEAR STATISTICS
WERE COLLECTED.

PROFESSORS SAY "MORE RESEARCH NEEDS TO BE DONE."

CONTINUE ON PAGE 16.

Yes, it's possible that nothing else is possible.

The common conditions of organization life will continue to be with us.

As Tops, we will continue to be in situations which are very complex and for which we have overall responsibility.

As Bottoms we will continue to be in situations which are negative, which "higher-ups" could be fixing, and which they are not fixing.

As Middles, we will continue to be in situations in which others are drawing us into the middle of conflicts they are having with one another.

As Customers, we will continue to be in situations in which delivery systems fail to deliver satisfactorily.

These conditions will not go away.

The question is: What choices do we have in reacting to these conditions? Do we have any choice?

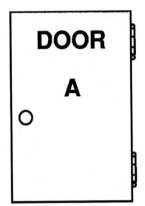 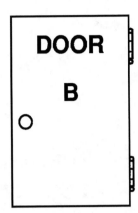

It is as if we are standing before two doors -- DOOR A and DOOR B.

When confronted with the predictable conditions of organization life,

we can choose to go through DOOR A

which will take us to the familiar disempowering scenarios of organization

life --

BURDENED

OPPRESSED

TORN

SCREWED.

Or we can go through DOOR B

which will take us to more empowering scenarios.

The problem is...

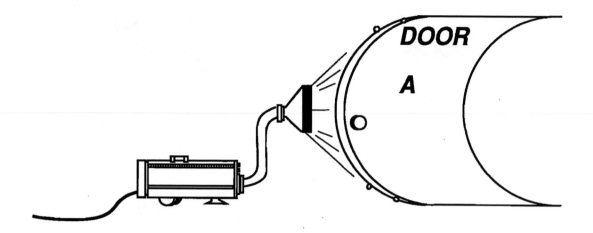

DOOR A is like a high-powered vacuum cleaner.

Just be in the presence of the predictable conditions,

and we are pulled right through DOOR A --

SUCK IT UP

BLAME "THEM"

DISAPPEAR IN THE MIDDLE

HOLD "IT" RESPONSIBLE FOR DELIVERY.

Automatic

reflexive

without thought or choice or deliberation --

WHOOOSH! --

through DOOR A we go.

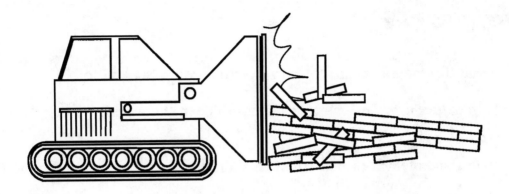

And DOOR B isn't really a door.

Someone came along and painted a door on a brick wall.

And there is no door here unless we come along with our bulldozer and

make a door.

But how do we create a door where there is no door?

We need to create DOOR B.

We do that by creating stands for ourselves regarding the kind of Top/Middle/Bottom/Customer we choose to be in the world.

We create stands which provide us with alternative ways of responding to the predictable conditions of organization life.

> If you don't want to be a Burdened Top,
>
> what is your stand regarding the kind of Top you do want to be?

> If you don't want to be an Oppressed Bottom,
>
> what is your stand regarding the kind of Bottom you do want to be?

> If you don't want to be a Torn Middle,
>
> what is your stand regarding the kind of Middle you do want to be?

> If you don't want to be a Screwed Customer,
>
> what is your stand regarding the kind of Customer you do want to be?

CREATING DOOR B FOR OURSELVES AS TOPS

TOP

**DOOR
B**

What if as Tops we NOTICE our tendency to suck up responsibility to ourselves?

What if we say NO to that tendency?

What new possibilities does that open up?

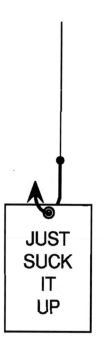

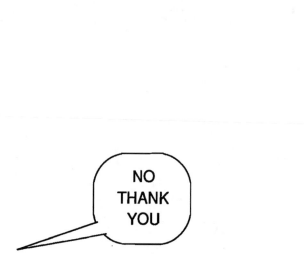

What if as Tops, instead of sucking up responsibility to ourselves,

we create a stand for ourselves regarding the kind of Top we want

to be in the world.

IN THE PRESENCE OF TOP OVERLOAD, MY BUSINESS AS A TOP IS

NOT TO SUCK UP AND SHOULDER ALL OF THE RESPONSIBILITY

FOR THIS OPERATION.

MY BUSINESS AS A TOP IS TO CREATE RESPONSIBILITY. MY

BUSINESS IS TO DO WHATEVER IT TAKES SUCH THAT

PEOPLE THROUGHOUT THIS ORGANIZATION

FEEL PERSONALLY RESPONSIBLE

NOT ONLY FOR THEIR CONDITION IN THE ORGANIZATION

BUT ALSO FOR THE CONDITION OF THE ORGANIZATION ITSELF.

Now, how do we do that?

How do we create responsibility in others?

The bad news is: We cannot create responsibility in others.

We cannot make them responsible.

The best we can do is create conditions

that make it possible for them to be responsible,

that encourage them to be responsible,

that support them in being responsible.

How do we do that?

First the commitment:

Is this the kind of Top you choose to be?

If your answer is yes,

then the appropriate strategies will show up.

For example...

Strategies for making possible, encouraging and supporting responsibility in

others:

◊ Involve others in the BIG issues you are facing. (Generally,
the more important the issue, the more likely we are to suck it up to
ourselves.)

◊ Ask for help.

◊ Share high quality information. (The more in the dark people
are about the system, the less likely they are to accept
responsibility for it.)

◊ Invest in the training and development of others. (If you
suck things up because you think you're the only one who can do
them, then invest in the development of others so that they can do
what now only you can do.)

◊ Create an enrolling vision for the system. Create a vision
of the system that captures others' energies, that presents it as
something of value in the world, something others want to be a part
of, something they want to contribute to.

◊ Invest in creating positive relationships with others. Be
the kind of person they want to support.

◊ Create powerful "games" for others to play. Carve out big
pieces of the action for others to run with; let them be Top of those
areas, and you be Coach.

◊ Create and use teams. Teams are a powerful source of
creativity. Create teams, and stay out of them. (At most, be Coach.)

◊ Reduce the differences between Tops and Bottoms. (It is
difficult for people to accept responsibility for the system when they
see mega-differences between themselves and Tops in terms of
perks, compensation, security, respect, and so forth.)

And,

if your commitment is to be a Top who creates responsibility in others,

you will forever be discovering new and better ways of doing that.

◊ This orientation to Top Overload is not natural.

◊ It is not something we do instinctively.

◊ It is not the human response to Top Overload.

◊ It is an orientation we have to create again and again, every time when, as Tops, we are experiencing overload.

◊ What is natural for us when we are experiencing Top Overload is to suck up all responsibility to ourselves.

◊ What is natural for us is to try out this new orientation and then abandon it because the predictable response is easier, more natural for us,

◊ or because this new orientation creates new challenges and problems we'd rather not face.

◊ Tops who create this more powerful orientation and operate out of it do not fall into the reality of BURDEN;

◊ they create very different realities

◊ in which there are very different problems and challenges to face

◊ and very different possibilities to explore

   for themselves

   for others

   for the situations they face

   and for their organizations.

CREATING DOOR B FOR OURSELVES AS BOTTOMS

BOTTOM

**DOOR
B**

What if as Bottoms we NOTICE our tendency to hand over to "THEM" responsibility both for our condition in the organization and for the condition of the organization?

What if we say NO to that tendency?

What new possibilities does that open up?

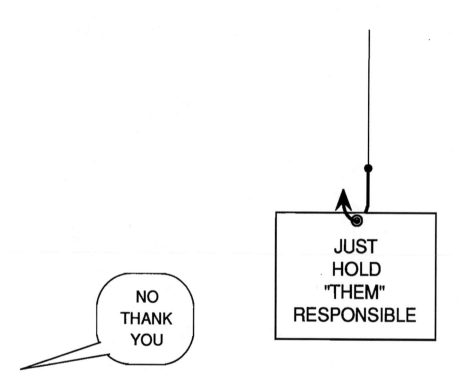

What if as Bottoms, instead of holding higher-ups responsible for

our condition and for the condition of the system,

we create a stand for ourselves regarding the kind of Bottom we

want to be in the world?

> IN THE PRESENCE OF BOTTOM DISREGARD, MY BUSINESS AS A
>
> BOTTOM IS NOT TO HAND OVER TO OTHERS RESPONSIBILITY
>
> FOR EITHER MY LIFE IN THIS ORGANIZATION OR THE LIFE OF
>
> THIS ORGANIZATION.

> MY BUSINESS AS A BOTTOM
>
> IS TO BE RESPONSIBLE FOR MY CONDITION IN THIS
>
> ORGANIZATION AND TO BE RESPONSIBLE FOR THE CONDITION
>
> OF THE ORGANIZATION.

> MY BUSINESS IS TO DO WHATEVER IT TAKES
>
> TO MAKE MY CONDITION IN THIS ORGANIZATION SECURE,
>
> SATISFYING, AND PRODUCTIVE,
>
> AND TO MAKE THIS ORGANIZATION SECURE AND PRODUCTIVE
>
> IN ITS ENVIRONMENT.

Now, how do we do that?

How do we accept responsibility for ourselves and the system?

We just do it.

When we are feeling Bottom -- regardless of how "high up" we are

in the system --

we feel at the mercy of problems.

It is as if problems are "out there"

and we have no part in creating them.

They happen to us.

We are the poor helpless suffering victims of them.

When, as Bottoms, we pass through DOOR B,

we see ourselves not as the victims of these problems

but as the CO-CREATORS of them.

We see ourselves as playing some part in the perpetuation

of these problems.

We see that these problems persist because of things we do

or don't do,

and that if we changed what we did

we might be able to make these problems go away.

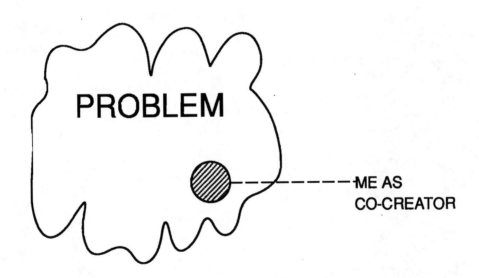

How do we do that?

First the commitment:

Is this the kind of Bottom you choose to be?

If your answer is Yes,

then the appropriate strategies will show up.

For example...

Strategies for being an empowered Bottom:

◊ Don't waste your energy blaming others.

◊ If something is wrong, fix it or

◊ do whatever it takes to get it fixed.

◊ Don't count on "higher-ups" to make things better.

◊ Remember: "Stuff" happens. Someone is always going to screw
things up. You can count on it. Don't get hooked on their "stuff."
Stay focused on making happen what you think has to happen.

◊ Be persistent.

◊ Respect yourself and

◊ don't let others treat you with disrespect.

◊ Don't be the Lone Ranger. Going it alone makes for fine drama
but poor change strategy. Who are your potential allies? Put together
powerful support networks.

◊ Be strategic. Take others' worlds into account. Accomplish
what you need to accomplish by easing the conditions of others.

And if your commitment is to be a Bottom who is responsible for your

condition and for the condition of the whole system,

you will forever be discovering new and better ways of doing that.

◊ This orientation to Bottom Disregard is not natural.

◊ It is not something that we do instinctively.

◊ It is not the human response to Bottom Disregard.

◊ It is an orientation we have to create again and again, every time when, as Bottoms, we are experiencing disregard.

◊ What is natural for us, when we are experiencing Bottom Disregard, is to hold "THEM" responsible for our condition, and to hold "THEM" responsible for the condition of the organization.

◊ What is natural for us is to try out this new orientation and then abandon it because the predictable response is easier, more natural for us

◊ or because this new orientation creates new challenges and problems we'd rather not face.

◊ Bottoms who create and operate out of this more powerful orientation do not fall into the reality of OPPRESSED;

◊ they create very different realities

◊ in which there are very different problems and challenges to face

◊ and very different possibilities to explore

for themselves,

for others,

for the situations they face,

and for their organization.

CREATING DOOR B FOR OURSELVES AS MIDDLES

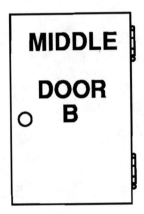

What if as Middles we NOTICE our tendency to lose our selves in

the middle of other people's issues and conflicts?

What if we say NO to that tendency?

What new possibilities does that open up?

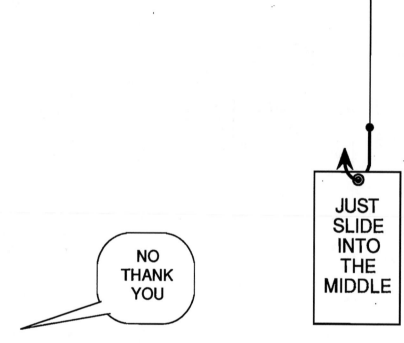

What if as Middles, instead of disappearing in the middle,

we create a stand for ourselves regarding the kind of Middle we

want to be in the world.

IN THE PRESENCE OF MIDDLE CRUNCH, MY BUSINESS AS A

MIDDLE IS NOT TO DISAPPEAR IN THE MIDDLE OF OTHER

PEOPLE'S ISSUES AND CONFLICTS

AND LOSE MY INDEPENDENCE OF THOUGHT AND ACTION.

MY BUSINESS AS A MIDDLE

IS TO MAINTAIN MY INDEPENDENCE OF THOUGHT AND

ACTION, AND TO EMPOWER MYSELF AND OTHERS.

Now, how do we do that?

How do we as Middles maintain our independence of thought and action and

empower ourselves and others?

First, the commitment:

Is this the kind of Middle you want to be in the world -- one who

maintains your independence of thought and action?

If your answer is Yes,

then the appropriate strategies will show up.

For example...

Strategies for being an empowered Middle:

◊ Be the LEADER.

Be the Top when you can, and take the responsibility of being Top.

Notice how often you make yourself Middle when you could be Top.

> Two Middles come away from the Top's office.
>
> Door A Middle says, "We didn't ask her if we could do such and such. Let's go back and ask."
>
> Door B Middle says, "We didn't ask, and she didn't tell us. Why don't we decide, not as an act of rebellion but because we're closer to the situation and have a better feel for what will work best."
>
> Door A Middle doesn't like that idea. "What if we do the wrong thing?"
>
> Door A Middle wants to ask for permission (and be Middle).
>
> Door B Middle wants to take the lead (and the responsibility of leadership) and if Tops don't like it, to ask for forgiveness.

Be a Middle who doesn't lose yourself in the middle -- who maintains your

independence of thought and action, who empowers yourself and others.

Be the Top when you can -- the LEADER -- and take the responsibility of being

Top.

◊ Be the REALITY CHECK

Be the Bottom when you should.

Some Middles describe themselves as SEWER PIPES.

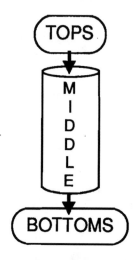

"Tops give us garbage to pass down and we just mindlessly pass it down. And then the garbage backs up all over us.

"Tops don't think they're passing down garbage. They think it's gold. But we're closer to the situation, and if we were paying attention, we'd know that that so-called 'gold' was really garbage."

Be the REALITY CHECK for Tops.

If it looks like garbage, don't pass it down.

Work it out with the Tops. Let them know how you see it.

The buck stops at the Top; the garbage stops in the Middle.

Be a Middle who doesn't lose yourself in the middle -- who maintains your

independence of thought and action, who empowers yourself and others.

Be the Bottom when you should, the REALITY CHECK.

◊ Be the COACH

Notice how often you do for others what they could be doing for themselves.

In the Middle, you do not have to dance to every tune that is called.

◊ Sometimes you coach others to do for themselves because you don't have what they want.

Be empathic -- "I understand that this is important to you."

Be committed -- "I want you to have a fair shot at getting it."

Be firm -- "But I won't get it for you."

Be coach -- "What I will do is work with you to help you develop the best strategy for getting what you want."

◊ And sometimes you coach others to do for themselves just because you think it's important for them to have the experience.

Sometimes you coach Bottoms to deal with Tops.

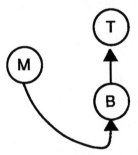

And yes, sometimes you coach Tops to deal with Bottoms.

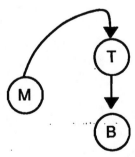

Be a Middle who doesn't lose yourself in the middle -- who maintains your independence of thought and action, who empowers yourself and others. Don't do for others, COACH them to do for themselves.

◊ Be the FACILITATOR

Notice how often you stand between people who ought to be together.

Here is Middle (M) between the Customer (C) and the
Producer (P).

Customer tells Middle what Customer wants.
Middle tells Producer what Customer wants.
Producer has a question about what Customer wants.
Middle asks Customer the question.
Middle brings Customer's answer to Producer.
Producer says "That wasn't what I wanted to know. What I really
wanted to know was..."
Middle brings Producer's question to Customer.
Customer gives Middle the answer and says "By the way, my
specifications have changed."
And on and on and on it goes.

This is what is often experienced as an important job -- on the phone all the
time, in meetings, needed by both sides.

Be a Middle who stays out of the middle,

be the Facilitator.

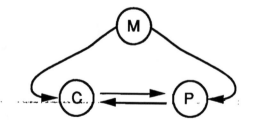

Bring together those people who need to be together and do what it takes to

make their interactions with one another as productive as possible.

◊ This orientation to Middle Crunch is not natural.

◊ It is not something that we do instinctively.

◊ It is not the human response to Middle Crunch.

◊ It is an orientation we have to create again and again, every time when, as Middles, we are experiencing crunch.

◊ What is natural for us is to lose our selves in the middle of other people's issues and conflicts, to lose our independence of thought and action.

◊ What is natural for us is to try out this new powerful orientation and then abandon it because the predictable response is easier, more natural for us

◊ or because this new orientation creates challenges and problems we'd rather not face.

◊ Middles who create and operate out of this more powerful orientation do not fall into the reality of TORN;

◊ they create very different realities

◊ in which there are very different problems and challenges to face

◊ and very different possibilities to explore,

for themselves,

for others,

for the situations they face,

and for their organization.

CREATING DOOR B FOR OURSELVES AS CUSTOMERS

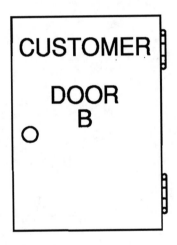

What if as Customers we NOTICE our tendency to hand over to the

delivery system responsibility for delivering the products or

services we want?

What if we say NO to that tendency?

What new possibilities does that open up?

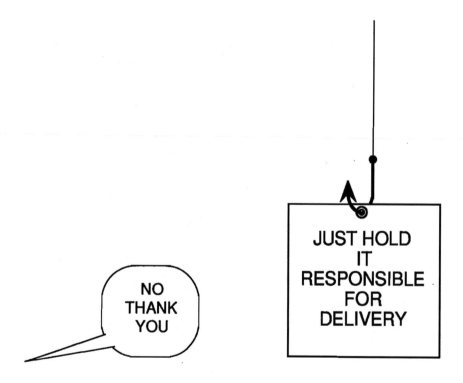

What if as Customers, instead of staying aloof and holding

delivery systems responsible for delivery,

we create a stand for ourselves regarding the kind of Customer we

want to be in the world?

MY BUSINESS AS A CUSTOMER IS NOT TO HAND OVER TO THE

DELIVERY SYSTEM TOTAL RESPONSIBILITY FOR PROVIDING ME

WITH THE PRODUCTS AND SERVICES I WANT.

MY BUSINESS AS A CUSTOMER IS TO DO WHATEVER IT TAKES

TO ENABLE PROVIDERS TO PROVIDE ME WITH THE QUALITY

PRODUCTS AND SERVICES I WANT FROM THEM.

I DO THIS NOT BY STAYING ALOOF FROM THE DELIVERY

PROCESS,

AND NOT BY COMPLAINING ABOUT THAT PROCESS,

BUT BY GETTING INTO THE MIDDLE OF THAT PROCESS

AND DOING WHATEVER IT TAKES TO MAKE IT POSSIBLE AND

EASY FOR THAT PROCESS TO WORK FOR ME.

Now how do we do that?

How do we get in the middle of delivery processes and help them

work for us?

First, the commitment:

Is this the kind of Customer you want to be in the world, one who accepts your responsibility in getting the service you want?

If your answer is Yes,

then the appropriate strategies will show up.

For example...

Strategies for being an empowered Customer:

◊ Don't stay aloof from the delivery system. Understand how it works so you will know the leverage points for helping it serve you.

◊ Set clear demands, standards, expectations.

◊ Avoid righteousness. The Customer position is an easy place in which to nurture righteousness -- how screwed up they are and how innocent you are. Keep focused on how you are going to get the delivery you want.

◊ Keep the thought: If you don't get the service you want, what are you doing wrong?

◊ Get involved in the production process early as a partner and not when it is too late as a judge.

◊ Stay close to the producer. Avoid intermediaries.

◊ Let the system know the kind of Customer you want to be. If they can't accommodate that style, move on.

And if your commitment is to be a Customer who gets in the middle

of delivery processes and helps them work for you,

you will forever be discovering new ways of doing that.

◊ This orientation to Customer Neglect is not natural.

◊ It is not something that we do instinctively.

◊ It is not the human response to Customer Neglect.

◊ It is an orientation we have to create again and again, every time when as Customers, we are experiencing neglect.

◊ What is natural for us, in the presence of Customer Neglect, is to blame the delivery system for non-delivery, and hold ourselves as blameless.

◊ What is natural for us is to try out this more powerful orientation and then abandon it because the predictable response is easier, more natural for us

◊ or because this new orientation creates challenges and problems we'd rather not face.

◊ Customers who create and operate out of this more powerful orientation do not fall into the reality of SCREWED;

◊ they create very different realities

◊ in which there are very different problems and challenges to face

◊ and very different possibilities to explore,

◊ new possibilities for themselves,

for others,

for the situations they face,

and for the organizations they are dealing with.

◊ It is clear that there is a choice.

It's DOOR A

or DOOR B.

We can fall into the familiar disempowering realities of organization life,

or we can create more powerful realities.

We can make the predictable responses to the common conditions of organization life

or we can create new stands for ourselves.

We can take the organizational world we get

or we can create the organizational world we want.

These are not small potatoes choices.

They take us through very different doors

and into fundamentally different worlds.

DOOR B requires of us more than slight modifications in behavior;

It calls for a fundamental shift in our way of being in the organization.

◊ A Top who uses the complexity in his or her world as an

opportunity to create responsibility in others is being

fundamentally different from

◊ Tops who react to these same conditions by sucking up

responsibility to themselves.

◊ A Bottom who responds to organizational problems by doing whatever it takes to see that these problems are handled is being fundamentally different from

◊ Bottoms who react to these same problems by laying responsibility for them onto others.

◊ A Middle who maintains one's independence of thought and action

  in the middle is being fundamentally different from

◊ Middles who lose themselves in the middle of other people's

  issues and conflicts.

◊ A Customer who deals with delivery systems by getting into the middle of the delivery processes and doing whatever it takes to help delivery systems work the way they are supposed to work is being fundamentally different from

◊ Customers who stand outside delivery systems -- hoping, blaming, complaining, or slipping into resignation.

What we are doing here is not only transforming organizations; we are using the everyday conditions of organization life as occasions for shifting our way of *being* in the world.

In these shifts there is new power, there are new productive possibilities, and there are new challenges for us as human beings.

To know the possibility of transformation is to experience the end of innocence:

> THERE IS CHOICE NOW WHERE BEFORE WE MAY HAVE THOUGHT WE HAD NO CHOICE.

It is not an unmixed blessing.

There is great power in creating the realities we want...

PEOPLE ARE MORE COMMITTED TO THEIR WORK.

THERE IS MORE INNOVATION.

HIGHER QUALITY PRODUCTS AND SERVICES.

DEEPER SATISFACTION.

A SENSE OF BELONGING.

LOYALTY.

MORE OPPORTUNITIES TO FEEL VALUED.

RESULTS.

CREATIVITY.

BUY-IN BY EVERYONE.

MORE RESPONSIBILITY THROUGHOUT THE SYSTEM.

PRODUCTIVITY AND PROFIT.

YOU'RE NOT A LOSER.

HIGHER MORALE.

ADAPTABILITY.

MORE PEOPLE FEELING LIKE THEY ARE IN THE DRIVER'S SEAT.

YOU GET WHAT YOU WANT.

THE POSSIBILITIES ARE UNLIMITED.

There is also a price to pay...

◊ It is not easy for us as Tops to give up the experience of

ourselves as being burdened by heavy responsibility and immense

complexity. It is not easy for us to accept the possibility that we do not

have to be burdened, and that we play a central part in whether or

not we are burdened.

◊ It is not easy for us as Bottoms to give up the experience of

ourselves as being oppressed by insensitive or malicious or

incompetent higher-ups. It is not easy for us to accept the possibility

that we do not have to feel oppressed by them, and that we play a

central part in whether or not we are oppressed.

◊ It is not easy for us as Middles to give up the experience of

ourselves as being torn apart by others. It is not easy for us to accept

the possibility that we do not have to be torn by them, and that we

play a central part in determining whether or not we are torn.

◊ It is not easy for us as Customers to give up the experience

of ourselves as being screwed by inflexible or ineffective

organizations. It is not easy for us to accept the possibility that the

delivery system could be delivering satisfactorily and that we play a

central part in whether or not that happens.

◊ IT IS NOT EASY FOR US AS HUMAN BEINGS

TO GIVE UP EXPERIENCING OURSELVES AS

THE WELL-INTENTIONED, HELPLESS, BLAMELESS,

POWERLESS VICTIMS OF OTHER PEOPLE OR

CIRCUMSTANCES.

◊ IT IS NOT EASY FOR US AS HUMAN BEINGS

TO ACCEPT THE CENTRAL PART WE CAN PLAY

IN DETERMINING HOW LIFE IS GOING TO BE

FOR US IN THE ORGANIZATION.

And yet this is what stands between the realities we fall into

and the realities we create,

between the story that happens with great regularity

and a new story --

one that is more empowering of us, others, and our

organizations.

BE A TOP WHO CREATES RESPONSIBILITY THROUGHOUT THE
ORGANIZATION.

BE A BOTTOM WHO IS RESPONSIBLE FOR YOUR CONDITION
IN THE ORGANIZATION AND FOR THE CONDITION OF THE
ORGANIZATION.

BE A MIDDLE WHO STAYS OUT OF THE MIDDLE -- WHO
MAINTAINS YOUR INDEPENDENCE OF THOUGHT AND ACTION, AND
WHO EMPOWERS YOURSELF AND OTHERS.

BE A CUSTOMER WHO GETS IN THE MIDDLE OF DELIVERY
PROCESSES AND HELPS THEM WORK FOR YOU.

SUMMARY

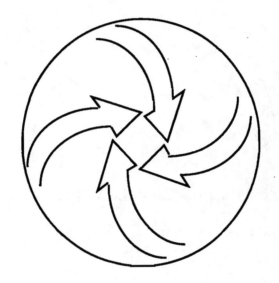

There is a story that develops with great regularity.

It is the story of an organization struggling to survive and develop in its environment.

In this organization there are the Tops, the Middles, and the Bottoms.

And in this organization's environment, there are its Customers.

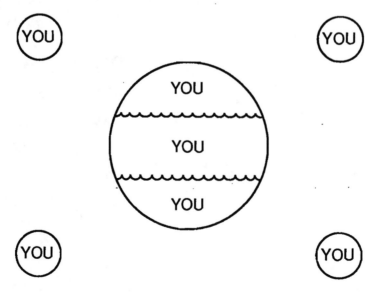

There are three possibilities available for this organization ...

POSSIBILITY I. INTERNAL WARFARE. We can misunderstand one another's worlds; we can misinterpret one another's behavior; we can see malice, insensitivity, and incompetence behind one another's actions; we can see ourselves as the well-intentioned, blameless, helpless victims of other people and of circumstances; we can act accordingly and go to war with one another.

POSSIBILITY II. UNDERSTANDING AND ACCOMMODATION. We can see into, comprehend, accept and adjust to one another's worlds; we can accommodate to others, acting in ways that make it possible, easy even, for them to do what we need them to do in order for us to move ahead with our work; we can see the "stuff" that comes at us from others as the behavior of people struggling to cope with and survive in the unique conditions of their worlds; we can choose NOT to get hooked on that stuff; we can stay in the Center Ring and not get drawn off into the drama of the Side Show; we can accomplish our goals by easing the conditions of others.

POSSIBILITY III. TRANSFORMATION. We can refuse to accept and accommodate to the familiar realities; we can say NO to the predictable responses to the common conditions of organization life; we can create new responses and new, more powerful realities in which as Tops we are not burdened, as Bottoms we are not oppressed, as Middles we are not torn, and as Customers we are not screwed. We can become central to creating what our organizational lives will be.

These are all possibilities.

And we do have a choice.